Senya
without you
have had
to learn anything I learnt

Ksenia Bure was born in Latvia, when it was still part of the Soviet Union and lived in Latvia until the age of 13, before attending Clifton College boarding school, in the UK. Without speaking English at first, transition to UK was an experience and it was not the last time Ksenia had to make cultural adjustments. As part of her Bachelor degree, German with Management studies, in University College London, Ksenia lived a year abroad in Germany, learning German and writing a dissertation on Jewish Survivors living in Berlin. Upon graduating, Ksenia joined Bloomberg LP and has worked in both London Headquarters and relocated to New York, covering different territories. Ksenia has worked at Bloomberg for 14 years, currently running its EMEA Data and Technology Sales business. Ksenia is married and has a daughter residing in London.

Mancey an, Thank you for your
friendship

Best
Ksenia
x

Dedicated to Beila…

Ksenia Bure

PRACTICAL MANAGEMENT SKILLS

AUSTIN MACAULEY PUBLISHERS™

LONDON • CAMBRIDGE • NEW YORK • SHARJAH

A CIP catalogue record for this title is available from the British Library.

ISBN 9781398432635 (Paperback)
ISBN 9781398432642 (ePub e-book)

www.austinmacauley.com

First Published 2022
Austin Macauley Publishers Ltd®
1 Canada Square
Canary Wharf
London
E14 5AA

First and foremost, I would like to thank my Father **Grigorij**, for instilling a belief in me, "one can do anything and should strive for success, no matter what gender or background you may have". His entrepreneurial spirit and work ethic has been imprinted in me as part of my DNA from birth, thank you.

Not surprising of course, that the man I married is a genius entrepreneur with the most analytical and creative mind combined, which is so seldom the case. **Boris**, thank you for being by my side, inspiring me to take things in my own hands, not giving up and believing in myself. You inspire and teach me how to be entrepreneurial on a daily basis and in part this book is my way of showing what I have learned from you. Boris's determination and love for achieving and success is so infectious, it continuously feeds my ambitions as well, thank you Boris, my love for you strengthens day by day.

I would like to also thank my sisters, **Daria, Anna** and **Sabina** for believing in me, encouraging me along and being my biggest fans.

Luck and right timing is often cited as driving components behind people's success, whilst that is also very true behind my career, mentorship and coming across the right people has also been one of the greatest components of my journey and the success that I have had. To that, I wanted to thank my first ever and now lifelong mentor, **Emiliano Santi** for believing in me, guiding me, listening and supporting me in all aspects of my life. Emi's wisdom and ability to see problems in the way no one does has acutely helped me. Secondly, I wanted to thank **Andrea Mosconi**, a manager that took me by surprise, someone I learned a great deal from, particularly from his endless enthusiasm, empathy, support but above all, for teaching me how to enjoy today, how to plan today for success tomorrow without getting carried away by tomorrow. Thirdly, I am a strong believer that you learn from every manager you have, I have been fortunate to have many great managers and one that I would like to particularly thank is, **Layne Moskowitz,** thank you Layne for your strong communication style, for your ability to inspire and always finding time to listen to me and to challenge; always with humour I dearly enjoy.

Last but not least **Adeem Altaf**, from the beginning of my career you have taught me so much from market knowledge, to people management to how to win people over; I see you as such a role model on how to develop talent, on how to advance careers and on how to build strong relationships with people; thank you for being you, never lose your energy and thank you for all your guidance. Throughout my career, I have had people take risks on me, without such risks my career could have taken a very different route, **Ian Yeulett**, in particular, has done so on many occasions with my New York move and other projects that have helped me grow; thank you for your continuous support Ian.

Coming across an editor **Jon Peacock** was by luck and I am grateful for the ease of our collaboration and the help he has provided me.

Finally, the light of my life, you may not know this today but **Beila**, you have been the inspiration behind this book. To leave a legacy behind for you, to share with you what mummy does at work and what one day I hope will be useful to you too. I love you endlessly.

Table of Contents

Introduction

I started writing this book to help people succeed in management roles. I have been a manager for longer than I have been a mother and a wife. Thankfully, there is no annual performance review on how well you are doing as a partner, parent, friend, or sibling – yet you are constantly evaluated when you are a manager. At the same time, many managers, especially new managers, struggle to handle everything that the role requires. They can often find themselves wondering how they ended up there, feeling lost, and thinking "I never thought it would be like this" – I know I did! So why are many managers so unprepared – and if that includes you, what can you do about it? Most management promotions occur organically after an individual has performed well for several years. These are workers that hit their targets year after year, good team players who understand and engage with the company's culture and have repeatedly demonstrated the skills and experience needed to do their job well. From my experience, very few of these high performers accept or seek promotion to management roles because they have the ambition to lead a team. Instead, many see the move up to managerial roles merely as the logical next step in their career; a step that provides higher status and higher earnings, and one which may entail more work and responsibility, but which is not essentially too different from the job they were doing so well before. However, very often when a high performer is taken out of her role without the right support, quite the opposite happens. Not only does the company lose the high performance that the new manager brought to their previous role, but if they struggle as managers, the change also creates a disorganised, demotivated, and unhappy team.

I know I felt this way about my first steps into management in 2010. My managers took a chance on promoting me because they hoped that, as a high performer, I would be able to somehow transform the entire team in my image, duplicating my achievements and output in each team member.

Taking a chance on promoting someone is the right thing to do because that's when we uncover talent. Indeed, finding and rewarding talented people is what differentiates successful companies from others. However, talent alone is not enough. I believe that without certain knowledge of experience-based management techniques, and practical guidance, it is all too easy for even the most talented, well-intentioned new manager to fail.

Over the last decade, I have led eight different teams, working in three different countries, and reporting to four different managers. Although nowadays I see myself as a good manager, I have learned the hard way that success doesn't come without making mistakes and learning from them. Throughout these years I read many different managerial books and took something from all of them. What I never found, however, were those practical examples that would have helped me recognise and manage the different types of issues I encountered. Above all, knowing then what I know now would have helped me win people over, and build that winning team, so much faster. The goal of this book is to do exactly that; by the end of the book, I hope to have passed on the most important things I learned in my career so that you don't have to work it all out for yourself. I must add, however, that no one situation is the same as any other. That's the beauty of management, every story involves people from different backgrounds with different histories and personalities that make your interactions different and unique.

So, what are these hard-learned lessons I intend to pass on? It is crucial to understand what the metrics are that make you a successful manager. How these metrics are measured and prioritised varies between different companies and industries, yet there are some universal constants: the ability to build a strong team, retain talent, develop people, gain respect, manage up and be a good manager to other leaders. Therefore, my advice on achieving these key goals will make up the backbone of this book. I will go through each of these metrics to help you uncover what it takes to succeed as a manager.

1 – Where to Begin – The Vital First 90 Days

The importance of the first 90 days at a new role is a familiar concept, highlighted by many managerial books. I particularly like this message from Michael Watkins' *The First 90 Days*:

> *"The actions you take during the first three months in a new job will largely determine whether you succeed or fail. If you fail to build momentum during your transition, you will face an uphill battle from that point forward."*

I, therefore, want to share my practical thoughts on your first 90 days, as well as talking about some experiences I lived through. Perhaps these insights can help prevent you from making unnecessary missteps during this crucial period. As mentioned in the introduction, I have led eight different teams during my career. Each team you lead represents an opportunity to reinvent yourself as a manager – or at least to apply any previously received feedback and learn from any mistakes you may have made in previous roles. If you are a new manager, as I too was once upon a time, where you tend to start is remembering what you liked and what you didn't in your managers. Writing these attributes down may help you visualise what type of a manager you would like to be, which could be an easy and useful first step when preparing for your role. What tactics did your managers use that made you feel valued, and conversely, what didn't they do that you wish they had? I believe that every manager has their strengths and weaknesses and, just like your interactions with any person, you want to learn and improve from their strengths and try not to dwell on the weaknesses. There are two types of managerial promotions: either you are promoted within your team, or you become a manager of a new team. The big difference of course is the degree to which your team already knows you or not. You may be well known for your individual contributions albeit not as a manager, or you may be an entirely unknown quantity to them. Your promotion may also mean that you are not just new in that specific role but facing a brand-new experience for you in a brand-new company. Each of these scenarios brings its own challenges, and this chapter aims to get you ready for every one of them. Do not underestimate the need to prepare for your role and the importance of those first 90 days. There is a well-known saying, "Don't judge a book by its cover" – similarly, don't jump to quick conclusions based on any negative first impressions of your new team. Take some time to understand why things are done the way they are, is there a back story as to why? Nobody likes to be criticised, even constructively; and criticism is particularly hard to take from a newcomer. Giving people the benefit of the doubt is important in all your initial conversations. First impressions matter, and you do not want to rub someone the wrong way, as it will take you a long time to change any negative first impressions and you always want to start from a position of strength. To save yourself the time you want to be prepared. As another old saying goes, "if you fail to prepare, you had better prepare to fail."

My First (Mis)steps in Management

At the beginning of my managerial career, I was promoted to lead the team that I was already a part of. People knew me as a go-getter, someone who knew how to sell and who understood their job well. What they didn't know is what kind of a manager I would be. Would I have their back, and how much would I drive them to become better at their job? My goal when I started was to try and get everyone to work the way I did. In my mind, this would get them to be superstars, and reach their targets if they only worked hard. I believed that the more you put in, the more chance you will get results and become better at what you do. There is some truth in that of course, and some merit to this approach.

However, as we will see in Chapter 2's discussion of differences in motivation, not everyone is driven by the same things, and my mistake was assuming that what worked best for me would work best for everyone. What I didn't appreciate then was that not everyone wanted to work hard, not everyone was so determined to reach their targets. People like working at a pace and in a style, that they believe works best for them and unless you can convince them that another way would be better, it is hard for them to reach that conclusion for themselves. They may force themselves to work your way for a short time, out of respect for you or fear about their job security – but unless and until they genuinely buy into your suggestions, they won't be happy, and that won't be sustainable for long.

My approach saw me identify flaws in each person's working style and try and fix them. I thought that by 'fixing them' I felt I was making the team better and helping them that way. In hindsight, this was tough and demoralising for them to hear; my approach was all about focusing on someone's weak spots rather than celebrating successes or coaching up their strengths. I was too hands-on and was rightly perceived by the team as a micromanager. I didn't trust my people and found it difficult to let go of control. All these are obvious mistakes that were not sustainable, and which made people on the team dissatisfied and unhappy. Let's look at other approaches I should have taken, and how they can apply to different situations.

Where Should You Be After 90 Days

After some time as a manager, you should have made your mark on the team – 90 days is a good time frame for this. This could be a drastic change, getting new people on the team or moving some people out, or a minor change such as introducing a daily 15-minute morning briefing on the day's goals. Whether this is a team that you were in before being promoted or a new team, making it your own is important, and some change is most likely inevitable. There will always be things that you deem to be working well, and things you want to change. There may be people you feel are not pulling their weight or have been in their role for so long that new energy is needed. Either way, it will help you to bring people into the team yourself because of the personal loyalty that they will have for you – and you will need as many allies as you can get during this transitional time. Change is an interesting concept; some people fear change due to the uncertainty of what it means for them, but many welcome the opportunities it brings. Opportunities for people to prove themselves, to reinvent themselves, or to right their previous wrongs. For instance, if you had a run-in with an old manager, your new manager may not know or care about it and will instead develop their own view on who you are, based on their experiences of working with you.

The First 90 Days Managing the Team You Previously Worked In

Another obvious difference between being promoted within your own team and into a new team is that in the former case you should already have clear opinions about what your teammates are capable of, and some ideas about what you want to change in your team before you are promoted. In theory, therefore, you can make these changes quickly. However, it's important to make sure people within your team feel part of those changes; you do that by speaking to them and asking for their opinions around what's working, what's not, and why. When planning and implementing your changes, make sure you take any feedback from the team into consideration whilst planning these changes – and make sure they know it. That way, all your people will feel reassured that their opinions were included and valued in your decision-making. I did this by scheduling one-to-one meetings with each team member to clear the air. During this time, I laid out my proposed structure and goals going forward and persuaded them to buy into and adhere to this. That showed my team that I meant business and also established to everyone that my main goal as their newly promoted manager was to help them, and the team achieve their goals and thus be able to pay them more money at the end of the year.

To Friend or Not to Friend?

In my first managerial role, I was promoted from within my team, so straight away I faced the challenge of having to manage my peers. Previously, I had often travelled and stayed with these colleagues on work trips abroad, spending a lot of time with the team, and I had gotten close to them as people. Now, not only did I face the demands of a new role as manager, but I also had to quickly create that distance from my friends where you can gain respect and be listened to.

Six months into the job managing my old team, I carried out the 'Stop, Start, Continue' exercise (as will be described in more detail in Chapter 2, *Cultural and Personal Differences in Motivation*). My promotion had changed our relationships. I found out that not only were people unhappy with my style of management but also some felt that I had favourites on the team. This is a common problem for any manager who was promoted within their old team, most likely caused by the fact that they had previously been (or were perceived as being) closer to some colleagues before becoming a manager.

I tried to overcome this first by simply putting those friendships on hold at work. In an ideal world, you would hope that your friends and other teammates alike would understand that at work, you are their manager and that outside of work you could just pick up again as close friends. To my disappointment, this did not work for me. Going forward, therefore, I distanced myself from my old friends, and spent less time socialising and talking with them as intimately as I had, although we maintained cordial relationships with mutual respect. Happily, for me, when I later changed roles from being the manager of that team, I was able to reconnect and rekindle those intimate friendships. I do not believe that I favoured anyone on the team, indeed if anything I think I was actually tougher with my old friends to avoid any such (unconscious) favouritism, but I could not affect how others felt, and how the situation was perceived. As the manager, I had to focus on the feelings that my actions caused others to have. From what this experience taught me, if I was again promoted within my team, I will focus on understanding each person's motivations and strengths. This will help me to build up a deep team consensus behind my strategy, ensuring that they are happy to own it and follow it through.

To get the balance right, I find you can still have pleasant relationships and conversations with your team members about things outside of work. However, if you do this with one colleague, it is vital to act the same with others, to show consistency and head off any perception of favouritism. As a leader, if you have learned something on a personal level about every individual in your team (information volunteered in authentic interactions), that indicates that you're successfully maintaining a balanced approach to personal relationships with them all. These interactions will help you build that relationship that perhaps you didn't have when you were their teammate. The key is to ensure that your closest confidantes and your non-friend teammates alike all feel that they are included in decision-making. A good tip is to involve everyone in interesting projects that will ensure you spend a lot of time interacting with them.

Another important lesson here is how to provide constructive criticism to your friends who are team-mates. I did witness one leader on my team, Sammy, manage her team, retain her friendships and still be able to honestly deliver constructive criticism. The trick was not dwelling on the promotion but instead staying as they were and letting their relationship develop organically without trying to force or regulate any change. The key for Sammy was to make sure that everyone was treated equally. In one-to-one catch-ups, she queried progress and asked how she could be of help. In group meetings, Sammy ensured that everyone's experiences and input were given equal weight; she set common goals and priorities and got team buy-in for their execution. I asked one of Sammy's friends how she thought Sammy was able to achieve this balance, and I got her answer in the form of an example. She related how during one particular catch-up meeting when the friend/colleague was expressing dissatisfaction with a work decision, Sammy didn't jump into defending her position – instead, she outlined the rationale of the argument and then left it, saying "sleep on it and let's touch base tomorrow." As her friend pointed out, this was exactly the approach Sammy took when helping her make tough non-work decisions as a friend; giving her opinion, then advising her to think things over before jumping to conclusions. It worked well for them as friends, and the colleague realised it was the right approach for the work issue too. Every scenario is different, and all people are unique, but the moral of this example is that you can make a success of your management role within your own team without burning bridges with the friends you've built. Listen carefully, and do not assume that everyone can or should do their job the same way as you would; you as a manager need to adjust as much as your staff does to a new management style.

The First 90 Days in a Brand-new Team

If you were promoted into a new team, you will only be able to make changes after you spend some time listening to people, hearing your team members out but also listening to clients (internal and external) that the team covers. As already mentioned, it's best to not jump to conclusions very quickly. Collect a wide range of opinions before fixing your own. Remember, not everything has to be solved immediately. All eyes are on you, so weighing up your decisions before making them can be beneficial. In the first couple of weeks, book your one-to-ones with your team members, and ask them to take you out on their client meetings. Only after you have spent time with everyone in the office, and outside the office with the clients, will you be able to form fair opinions on each individual. Spend some time digging deeper into performance statistics and CRM data to see what quality of work the team members are operating with. During the time you spend shadowing your people, ask questions but don't criticise. It helps to formulate an open-ended question rather than demanding 'why' something happened, to avoid seeming accusatory. For instance, "how have we resolved this issue" or "are you aware of any developments in this particular area of the business?" Double-check your findings by asking similar questions to other colleagues. This is the way to build an accurate and well-rounded picture of them as individuals and workers. If it is a small team, it won't take a long time. If it's a team of say, 70 people, it may take longer – but you must make the time for a proper assessment of everyone within your group. This has helped me immensely as people appreciated the time I was taking and felt that I cared about really finding out about them, rather than just listening to my predecessors. The next step (probably 14-30 days after you start) is to gather everyone together to formally introduce yourself and share your initial thoughts and your overall plans for the first 90 days. This is your opportunity to impress your people. You can showcase your identity and the identity you want for the team, by sharing what's important, or even non-negotiable, for you. I spent a good 10 hours preparing for my first group address. It was the most important event for me because this was a chance to set the right tone for your group from the start. I started with a similar introduction as I had used during our one-on-ones, sharing my strengths and my values. I talked about my background and how I hoped to use my experience to lead the group to success. I then summarised key observations about the market before I moved on to outlining the initial findings from the conversations and client meetings. For the next 10-15 minutes, I spoke about operational expectations, things that the culture of the firm expected, and things that I would be monitoring, to make sure people knew what I would look at and provide everyone with an equal playing field. By being transparent from the start, people know what you are about, what you are looking for, and what they need to do to impress you. Remember, as a manager, you are only as strong as your weakest person, so it's vital that everyone understands what they need to do and why. I then spoke about the next 60-90 days and what I will be doing to build a relevant strategy and let them know that I would continue to ask questions to build up the full picture and would be choosing and assigning people to analyse certain business segments. I stressed that my goal in all my investigations was not to criticise but to obtain facts and opinions and that I would do that by listening to numerous voices. Over the previous couple of weeks, you probably had already made certain observations and strategic decisions for the group to follow. For those who are not able to join the dots, you outline what those strategic pushes have been and ensure people are all on board with the current group strategy. It's unlikely that you would dramatically change the overall strategy itself over the first 90 days or so because any strategy is built on the back of market conditions and product offerings; unless there have been absolute chaos and mismanagement before, the majority of this will most likely still be relevant. What is also constant are the expectations that your boss will have of you, which shouldn't have changed with your group unless you and your boss were both new in your roles, so they also are reassessing everything.

You should be candid with your group in this address, sharing the reality that part of your job is to pass on the big picture company line, but stress how you will do your utmost to ensure that the group will have your backing at a bigger table and that you will work to filter out all the unnecessary noise and prevent any unnecessary disruptions. I wouldn't explicitly tell them that you will be assessing everyone intending to lose some of them. I would say that changes are likely, and you appreciate that change can be scary for some, but I would also frame that by emphasising how changes bring new opportunities for people to succeed, and that you will be evaluating what these opportunities may look like for certain individuals on the team over the next 90 days.

90 Days in a Brand-New Firm

If you are hired into a new company, experiencing a brand-new team and new culture, then of course the job becomes that extra bit harder. You need to spend the full 90 days learning the ropes of the company and product for yourself. You need to speak to as many people as you can, build your product knowledge up quickly, and find the right advocates to who you can turn for subject matter queries. All this getting up to speed will take up all those 90 days (if not more) until you have built the right level of knowledge to sound credible when addressing the team. 90 days may seem like a long time; in reality, it is a heartbeat, particularly at a new firm. So, use those days wisely to build that knowledge of the market, product, people, and your understanding of management's expectations both for you and for your group. Within the new company, you want to build allies fast and make valid assessments of people. Speak to your peers to get a sense of how things worked before you joined and what complaints and strengths the people have. Learn who can you trust and especially, find out who else wanted your role. I would typically spend some time with those people. Some of them may have come close to getting your job ahead of you, and their experience, skills, and knowledge of the group may be very valuable – but be careful in case they have any bitterness against your or your bosses for not being chosen. Whether or not you think they are behind you, it's good practice to consider giving them an important role within your structure; you may not only help yourself by retaining their talent, but this will make them feel valued, and also enables you to keep an eye on them. Each situation at each company is quite different, and it's tough to offer you a ready-made script on how to recruit relevant allies. Nevertheless, it's important to still spend time with as many useful people as possible, with your peers, clients as well as adjacent departments, to build a 360 view of your company's infrastructure and form opinions on the operational capabilities of your group. Once that's done the rest will come with experience. It is also important to find out whether there are other recent external hires in the company. If so, it's a great idea to go for lunch with them to pick their brains on any tips on how to adjust to the company faster. In my experience, you will find that many things are done in a way that you will question or may find uncomfortable. Again, it is easy to jump in with both feet and start saying, "this doesn't make sense", "in our old firm we did that" and "my old way was better because of x, y, and z". I was guilty of doing that a few times when I went over to the US office and found myself confronted by a completely different managerial style with different practices. Now, it helped me that it was still the same firm, but what I learned is that no one likes a person who spoke one too many times about how they did things differently elsewhere. At times my insight was taken on board, and people valued the diverse perspective that I brought to the table, but that fresh perspective is best used sparingly and kept to yourself until people ask for your opinion, rather than being eagerly volunteered at every opportunity.

Gaining Decision-Making Power

Overall, getting on with the job is probably the right thing to do in a new environment, rather than highlighting or critiquing the weaknesses of the current system. Emphasising the strengths of the new firm will help you fit in and will also help you gain respect for its ways quicker, so I would generally recommend that new hires spend their time focusing on what you were employed to do. In companies where corporate culture is particularly strong, it may take some time before you learn how to adjust. In my experience, coming into a company where things are done in a certain way, particularly working with a non-standardised CRM, may mean that you are bogged down with pedantic operational matters that at first may seem very inefficient. Unless this is a start-up where decisions such as that may have been made by one person, there is a high chance that in a large well-established corporation, things are done the way they are for a reason. Spend some time understanding what that reason is before you let your frustration build up.

Of course, it may be the case that the reasons that you discover make little sense to you, and that may mean you may want to question further. In my opinion, there is always room for questioning – indeed, one of the biggest benefits of new hires is exactly that; they question current processes and may find holes that can be fixed. This is a clear benefit in theory, though politically, the people who built these processes may be very protective and not like it if you expose certain flaws with their current processes or the reasoning behind them.

I had the benefit of being on a six-month assignment where I was explicitly asked to do exactly this; to act as an external consultant and evaluate all the internal processes within my firm and probe for weaknesses and question the reasoning behind the original and existing build. This was an excellent experience, and I learned that all your investigations should be performed in the open. You want to ask the person to run through the original rationale behind the process, and not assume it will be how you understand it from your experience using the process yourself. if you still think things need changing after your original evaluation, instead of continuing to poke holes, you need to offer better solutions that may bring a better result than the current one. When or if you get to report your findings to senior management, make sure you come up with a presentation focused on the potential benefits of doing things in your different way, instead of just pointing out the flaws in the status quo. I presented my findings at the end of my six-month assignment, making certain that those findings were thoroughly vetted by other people before I presented them. It's important to test your ideas on other people beforehand so that you have the buy-in of others. In addition, if others start talking about it, perhaps some words of your ideas will even reach the ears of the decision-makers you are presenting to. This way, when it comes to your presentation, they won't be surprised and will have had a chance to think about the benefits – so there is a higher chance of them accepting your arguments.

Limits to Change

Of course, you may find that even if your ideas are valid and are beneficial, the company may not have the budget or free headcount to implement the changes. You find yourself competing with other internal projects with established sponsors that are already under way, leaving you in a frustrating position. Or you may also find that even though your suggestions are valid, and there is the managerial buy-in and even available resources to implement your ideas, the changes have an unforeseen negative impact on some different aspects of the business. Making a change, therefore, is taking a risk. Any large operational change also means changing the habits of the many people who were employed before you even got there, people who would all need to change the way they work. Purely in disruption terms, it is much easier to ask one single person (you) to swallow your reservations and adjust to existing ways, instead of one person's dissenting opinions changing how a whole department works. Focusing on the things you can control and not worrying about those you cannot is an art, and a great rule for any manager to live by. I find it useful also to accept that. In today's bureaucratic world, there are certain expectations, from your boss and the senior management, that you most likely won't have control over. A large part of a middle manager's job is passing messages down to their people while filtering and shielding them from certain irrelevant tasks. I would argue that middle managers are mainly executors of the wider strategy. Any group strategy will only deviate slightly from the overall departmental approach (I'd estimate around 10-15% leeway to adapt in sales, the area I know best), leaving little room for innovation. Thus, the way that middle manager makes a difference, is how they manage their group and get them to get the job done.

So, over these first 90 days, of course, you can and should look for things that are not working well structurally, but your time will be more effectively spent looking at the quality of your people and seeing whether you have the right talent in the right place – shuffling people, changing working teams around and firing or hiring as appropriate to end up with the right talent. The key is to ensure that you hire and retain the right people and (if you manage managers) coaching your leaders to lead in the right way. Who do you appoint to get the job done at a high quality? I maintain that having people who trust you and believe in you, is essential. People that you can motivate and will be receptive to your management.

All that in mind, I do believe that there is scope for questioning certain mandates within the firm and offering suggestions on how to do things differently. However, I also believe that many times, external hires, in particular, would succeed better by first embracing and adjusting to the ways of the new firm, before trying to change things. This initial adjustment may take a couple of years and indeed that's probably that's the minimum track record you can have under your belt with the firm before you are likely to be listened to. Only once you have established yourself and earned your peers' and bosses' respect, can you start shaking things up with any hope of being heard – and I'd recommend making these suggestions only once they have been weighed up and vetted by a few trusted peers.

2 – Cultural and Personal Differences in Motivation

One thing I found comforting when developing my managerial style is that no matter what your industry or what level of manager you are, the key learnings are universal, and the goal is the same – whether you are a team leader, middle manager, or regional manager, your role is to lead, organise and motivate the people under you and reach your targets. What I did find striking, however, was the importance of culture – how much managerial style had to be adjusted when managing, for instance, a team of Eastern Europeans instead of a team drawn from Western Cultures.

I am a big advocate of equality, diversity, and inclusion, but this doesn't mean that a 'one size fits all' approach is desirable or even possible. The approach you take and the considerations to remember when working with different people vary from case to case. One should not underestimate how different managing a woman can be from managing a man; likewise, your communication style will have to be adjusted when managing an Eastern European instead of an American. Even within the same gender or cultural grouping, there are still huge individual differences, and there are many psychological tests that a manager can take or give to see what type of a teammate they are dealing with – the go-getter or the analytical person, an extravert, or an introvert; different communication styles are optimal for each person. Because people are all different, situations and stress levels affect people with different backgrounds very differently, thus meaning that you never find yourself dealing with the same situation or the same issue twice. Dealing with this variety is a big part of why I love my job – it's never the same twice, and always challenging. Whatever the unique situation at hand, there are certain triggers to look out for that will help you make the right call on how best to manage it.

Status and Appearance in Eastern Europe

In my first role as a manager, I led a team of nine people, covering the old CIS region and Russia. To give you some background, my family was all born in the old Soviet Union and migrated to Latvia where I was born. Our native language is Russian, and although Latvia gained its independence in 1991, I have always considered myself a Russian speaker living in Latvia. It is my ability to speak Russian that enabled me to first be appointed team leader of a Russian-speaking team. Level of prestige, earnings, and appearances matter when leading a team in Russia and the former Soviet states, and the same applies throughout most of Eastern Europe. If a more junior team member has a Louis Vuitton bag and you have a shabby-looking old bag with a hole in, you will lose a degree of respect. Similarly, if a man had scuffed shoes or dirty cuffs, the same loss of face will apply. This is vastly different from managing a western European team, where clothes, accessories, even your appearance hardly matters, as long as you have the knowledge and a proven track record to win your colleagues' respect.

I found that as an inexperienced female manager, I had to take particular pains to look the part of a manager, to make sure I could gain the respect not only of my team but also of my clients (an experience which I think perhaps is not confined to any particular culture or heritage but speaks more to the global issue of gender inequality taking its toll). One example that I will never forget was the day that I wore my hair in a messy bun to a client meeting. This client (a middle-aged man with an expensive suit and watch), was a CEO of a bank, and I, the 25-year-old female team leader. I was introduced to him as the regional head of sales for my well-established company. As he looked at me, his eyes lingered a little longer on my head and I swear, he decided to himself there and then that my look was not respectable enough. Of course, I know this is just my interpretation of how he regarded me, and we cannot know for certain. Perhaps this was just the insecurities of a 25-year-old. However, what is certain is that he didn't spend long talking to me, nor did I ever subsequently manage to establish a rapport with him. This was very dissimilar to my experience with other CEOs that I have met previously, while I wore more suitable hairstyles and looked very professional, where I was easily able to collaborate with them. Even if his dismissive judgement was purely in my head, that in itself reflects how far the culture made us conscious of appearances. In subsequent cultural sensitivity training, I also heard that if you want to make a big sale and you know that the person you are meeting will be wearing a red tie, it will help your chances to make that sale if you too wore a red tie or some other apparel of a similar brand to theirs. In Russia, where women and men alike take more care over their appearances than arguably any other culture, it's no surprise that what would seem a superficial irrelevance in other places can make for an effective ice breaker that you can both point out and briefly comment on.

Conviction of Arguments and the Authoritarian Style

It is not just your appearance that is important when working with this type of culture but also the conviction with which you present your arguments and beliefs to the team. When I carried out a communication styles psychological test across our team (see Chapter 4 for more on these), I realised very quickly that every individual fell into the colour red type. This essentially meant competitive, fiery, ambitious, extraverted, speak-their-mind individuals who expect to be heard and demand a leader no less ambitious or competitive than themselves. If at any point in time you seem unsure or hesitant about something, the team feels it more so than with any other culture. Your hesitation can then be used against you, and you are opening yourself up to a potential power struggle with a person within your team that either wants your role for themselves or at the least, doesn't believe you are up to it. In the western world, such hesitation may be perceived as indicating a thoughtful and considered approach, but in Eastern Europe, if you don't give an immediate answer to something, you have come unprepared. This also is something that I learned for myself early in my managerial career. After I once hesitated to answer a question in a team meeting, I later overheard one rep say to another, "See, she doesn't even know the answer, so how can we be expected to know it ourselves?" Over time, I learned that this can be deflected by an answer like, "Well, this is an interesting question – and there are many facets to the answer, given that we need to consider [factors a, b, and c] and that we have to consult with [groups x, y and] …" This approach not only avoids the unpreparedness stigma of a hesitant or non-response, but it also gains you respect as a demonstration of how fully you understand all the complexities while leaving no suggestion that you can't answer the question. This slightly long-winded type of answer also buys you more time to think of how best to reply! Other than conviction, the style of management that you need when running a team of Eastern Europeans is an authoritative one. Now to western readers that may sound a bit too much like a dictatorship, but just as you need conviction in your voice when you speak, you also have to set clearly defined guidelines and structure to ensure that everyone follows your lead and that your goals are achieved. When reflecting on my and my family's experience working with Eastern European firms, the concept of coaching and the aim of motivating employees hardly exists – there is no 'carrot and stick' approach to managing individuals – just the stick[1]. People have a job, and they just need to get on with it. When

---

[1] For anyone unfamiliar with the 'carrot and stick' concept of management' it is a metaphor for positive and negative reinforcement, whereby you reward someone for doing a good job (giving the donkey a carrot) or alternatively tell workers off or even scaring them with disciplinary action (threatening the donkey with a stick) for poor performance.

managing in former Soviet Union regions, it was effective for me to elevate one high-performing person's performance in front of their peers, as praising them in front of others made the other people in that team feel special and loved – that was their 'carrot'. In America, when I tried that, I often received the feedback that it was perceived as favouritism to that individual, and that if one were to speak positively about one person you need to think additionally about how to award the entire team. People responded to the carrot of face-to-face praise on a one-to-one basis very differently there than in Russia. There, these meetings had been task-based, all about 'this is what needs doing, what have you done on specific tasks and what are you doing this week'. In America by contrast, it was about the performance and development of the individual – what I saw that was good in this person's work, and how we can improve on other aspects. Using this supportive 'carrot management' is not ideal for managing Russians, as very often it can cause complacency and allow arrogance to develop but using the authoritarian 'stick management' approach in America may cost you your job and your team. When I moved to America for an assignment after running an Eastern European team, I was perceived as a dictator, giving others no room to breathe. The stick approach I was used to simply didn't work in that culture and I had to quickly react to feedback and adapt my style to win the team over.

Being Self-aware

An important lesson I learned then is – you have got to be self-aware and be open to feedback and criticism of your approach. It doesn't matter if you think as a manager you did everything right; the key is how your actions are making others feel. If your actions provoke negative feelings, it is you that needs to rethink your approach and change these actions to get a different reaction. As Isaac Newton once said, "Every action has a reaction." Any strategy, any conversation you have as a manager has someone on the other end reacting to it. They are entitled to that reaction, but you will only know exactly how that made them feel if you ask them and – crucially – if they feel they can open up honestly to you. This openness is not going to just happen, especially if you have not had the chance to build a level of trust yet, as you are the boss. So, you need to pre-empt any problems: think about these scenarios and talk them through with your peer or manager and try to predict through all different possible reactions to a situation – much like if you were playing chess, you would have to foresee what consequences could potentially come out from a move before you make it. Don't forget to factor in that person's background and personal situation to obtain the most realistic forecast of how they may react. What worked well for me, and how I discovered that my style of management wasn't working for me in America, was an exercise I ran with my team after three months in my role: what's working, what's not working, and what can we do more of. Some people call it 'Stop, Start and Continue'. This is hugely effective – but only if framed correctly and if you are not defensive in receiving this feedback. Your team may at first use this as an opportunity for a personal attack on you, so make sure to frame this exercise to be entirely about what's going on with your team, and why – not a referendum on you as a manager. You leave your team for an hour to do so and when you return you need to be open to listening. I noticed that my German team found this exercise especially useful and very practical, and with the English, a more diplomatic approach to providing feedback did kick in, with fewer explicit "what's not working" examples being offered. In that case, the solution is to draw attention to it, and try to draw people's hidden frustrations out gently with a smile – "Really? There has to be *something* that makes you feel, 'Oh if I was the manager I wouldn't do it like that.'" Never react by arguing out your reasoning behind why your way was the right way. This will make them feel that you had no intention of listening or changing, and maybe even that you are only trying to flush out troublemakers – this will just shut down any hope for future communication and trust. This defensive response would also defeat the whole point of the exercise, which is about how *they* feel, and how your actions impact the performance and feelings of your team members. For instance, if someone raises a bad communication style as one of the aspects that are not working, you need to ask for examples of when your communication failed and how it should be improved – how they would like to be talked to, for instance. One of my examples was that I sent out too many emails and that they would prefer to receive one email containing 3-4 action or information points in one go. That way they would be less on edge every time they saw my name pop up. I understood their need and was able to adapt to it.

Feedback in Different Cultures

When you understand the feedback and the reasoning behind it, it should then be simple to act on it. After another three months, arrange a check-in to see whether your team has noticed and appreciated the changes you have implemented since that first exercise. This would help win your respect, as nothing feels better for your team members than feeling listened to and included in improving the teams' overall performance. That's very motivating. Now, of course, some suggestions that get raised may be a non-negotiable no-go for you for good reasons. In that case, you need to patiently explain the reasoning behind that and get people to grasp why this is a non-starter for you.

One example I encountered was when working with a German team. I found that the men in particular needed confirmation that I was able to do their job as well or better than them. On one occasion, the reps called me out with the challenge, "When was the last time you did that yourself?" Managing from the front has always been part of my managerial style and for me, that includes never asking someone to do a job that I was unable or unwilling to do myself, so I did not flinch in telling them about how I had indeed recently done that job. However, I also let them know very clearly that the question, and the way it was presented, was confrontational, patronising, and undermining. I made sure they understood that this kind of response was unacceptable and that if they have a genuine query about something I've asked them to do, their approach should be more like "Why do these tasks need to be done", instead of this hostile form of push-back. This territorial squabble was very different from my experience in America where specialists were seen as an important component of a successful team, but not the be-all and end-all. It was how a manager was able to leverage a specialist that was celebrated, more so than the manager being expected to be an expert on everything – in other words, the manager was accepted as the 'specialist in management'.

Getting to Know the Team as People

What was heart-warming for me was how the Western Europeans valued a more personal touch in management than in America or Russia. My team expected me to know the names of their partners and kids and responded well when our one-to-ones began with a five-minute chat on family news and plans for the weekend. This was quite different to Russia or even America where it was all straight down to business and considered perfectly satisfactory to jump right into the meeting. With an Eastern European team, there will of course be some pleasantries, but certainly not knowing the names of each other's partners or children would be common. A big reason is a distance caused by seniority and rank (also a common concept elsewhere around the world), due to which team members don't often ask personal questions of you, and hence it is perhaps diplomatic for managers not to pry either. I believe, however, that you can build relationships and find out peoples' kids' names without prying, and people respond well and appreciate it.

In some parts of the world, in many Asian countries, pleasantries and relationship building are a huge part of doing business, as well-documented in *Shoe Dog,* the memoir of Nike founder Phil Knight. Knight recounts how he worked with Asian manufacturers, and how the relationship-building phase saw him flying out for numerous 'get to know you' meetings and spending significant time cementing alliances on a personal level to gain trust before any significant business deals took place.

Culture of Promoting Others

Something that I would recommend thinking about when taking over a team in North America is how often in the past you have helped someone to advance their career. In the USA, more than anywhere else, an aspect that was rated highly in a manager was their ability to promote others. People placed a lot of value in having a manager with a history of getting their people promoted. This of course is an important factor in any region, but I felt that this was especially accepted as a key criterion to desire from your manager in the US. However, interestingly, I also observed in America that there a considerable proportion of the workforce was not at all promotion-driven and saw it as perfectly acceptable to spend their career in one role, within one department, without progressing into the managerial ranks. A managerial role was seen by those individuals as an administrative burden that can only bring unnecessary extra headaches. Many organisations expect managers not only to sell themselves and hold down their accounts but also to manage a team and produce results. This to many is not attractive, especially if your company values meritocracy and is commission based. If you are a good performer that has a guaranteed bonus for reaching your targets, you may well be better off than a team leader or a manager, even though they are theoretically in the more senior role, as their compensation is heavily or wholly dependent on the performance of the whole team. Managers in America do receive an elevated level of respect because they have gone through the ranks for a long time themselves before proving themselves and becoming managers. This is not necessarily the case in Europe, where there is more likelihood of a person being promoted quicker at a global company because of a language, culture, or another specific skillset that sets them apart. In Europe, there is considerable diversity in cultures, languages, and heritages rather than in America where other than Latino communities, there is a dominant homogenous American culture. European teams thus have a wider pool of talent to choose from and face more of a need to find these different managerial traits. Also, due to geographical closeness and ease of movement, European workers are more open to living and working in a foreign country and culture, and it is more common to see someone decide to look outside of – or return to – their home country when moving to a new role than it is in America. This is partly why in Europe our company had a less experienced set of managers than in America where they tend to stay in the same position for longer. Some firms also have a deliberate strategy of encouraging high turnover and thus using more junior managers – a youthful and inexperienced management team may bring new ideas, energy, and more diversity of experience into teams, and also of course they tend to be cheaper to employ and replace than a more senior group.

Managing Entrenched Long-Serving Colleagues

When managing different levels of seniority within the same team, a manager faces another set of challenges. When managing in America a couple members of my team were the same age as my father, and my managers too were typically of a similar age to my parents. When a 28-year-old manager is then presented to an older team, it's natural to feel an extra burden of proving yourself. This pressure or scrutiny may be self-inflicted or imaginary but without a doubt, this is a common scenario for many early-career managers to find themselves in. This is not an easy situation and you do need to think carefully about the tactics that you use to win senior members of your team over.

What has worked well for me is simply to try not to dwell on a persons' age or how long they have been in their role compared to me. Instead of trying to prove myself to them, I try to learn how they complement my skill set. I put the emphasis on what *I* bring to the table and what skills have gotten me into my role. Once I demonstrate how I have risen through the ranks, and how I can help my people develop those skills themselves, they usually see my arrival as an opportunity, not an insult. From there I can move on to look at the skills and experience my team members have, and how my skills complement these. I also make it clear that I will do what I can to help that person learn to do a better job, hit their targets, and hence get more money at the end of the year.

Overcoming Resistance

Of course, some people may still not necessarily rate you or the skills that you have demonstrated – they may still think that they have nothing to learn from you (or anyone) about doing their job, or that they would be a better managerial choice than you. Alas, this stubborn resistance is not limited to older or longer-standing colleagues. Navigating this tricky situation is a matter of not only proving yourself over time but also understanding what motivates your team members. This is true across each culture. Very often managerial books talk about figuring out what motivates each individual. When you understand that, then building rapport with that individual and helping them get the job done becomes that much easier. For instance, senior people that have been doing their job for a long time are typically happy doing what they are doing and in no rush to get anywhere career-wise. These people have gotten into the habit of doing their job their way over the past however many years and trying to change them can be close to impossible. I am a true believer that you cannot change a person – this insight comes from my experience of personal relationships, as it does with many people. Thus, when you have an experienced person on your team who seems set in their ways, it will just cause conflict to try and force them to toe the line your way. In such a case, you need to find another method to get them on board. You can help to get them to feel valued by getting them to share their opinion with the team, or to recount what worked well for them in the past. It motivates them when you leave them to their own devices and indicates that you respect them for what they bring to the table. If the root of their resistance is that they are personally ambitious and covet your job, then delegation and sharing responsibility will do the trick in keeping them motivated. Let them take charge of one or two parts of your strategy or a specific (but non-vital) project. They will get the experience of management-level work and feel trusted – and you keep them too busy to take over or interfere with the rest of your management.

Managing Inertia

For an ambitious person like myself, it was hard to fathom that someone could be content to just do their job for 15 years, without any desire for further career advancement. I came across one of these people, Darren, in America. It was close to impossible to change his way of work, but what I quickly learned was that he didn't want, or need, to be changed. He did a good job servicing his clients and he was content with an annual inflationary pay rise. He was satisfied with his pay, and he didn't want to get any high-profile jobs that would raise his status but add to the scrutiny he was under. Darren already faced plenty of demands during his time having two teenage daughters, and he wasn't desperate for more money with a wife who had her own florist business. In addition, his commute to work took nearly two hours, so he had no interest in challenging new work or roles that would take up yet more time. My first thought was that I would be better off trying to replace Darren with some hungry new blood. However, I soon realised that there is room in a mature market for these senior account managers like Darren. He had built up several established and successful client relationships and was able to service clients on a day-to-day basis very well. He didn't have to be taught, he was no trouble, and he understood the company's culture. In a big organisation, there was room for someone like him and it helped to know that he respected me, and we worked well together. He knew that I mostly trusted him to get on with it, so whenever I did tell him that he needed to brush up on certain market developments he was happy to comply – he appreciated that I had good reasons for intervening and understood that I was not getting on his case just to prove myself or make a point. There are some similarities with the German market, where people are not motivated by money but by company loyalty and job security, which trade unions in Germany make sure of. If you have a team of inexperienced staff, the presence of a long-tenured consistent performer helps you steady the boat. Let's not underestimate how much more time you have to spend intensively managing and mentoring a recruit compared to an experienced employee, hence there is always a need for a veteran on a team whom you can trust to do a good job. This is just one example of the sort of call that you as a manager will make times daily looking at your people and understand who fits best where. You can decipher this by marrying each person's skillset to the relevant requirements of the job making sure to fit them into a role that will expose any weaknesses they have as little as possible. You're trying to allocate a job to someone that they can succeed in because, as a manager, you are only as strong as your weakest teammate. Another key consideration is offering people a role doing what they enjoy most (if they can do so effectively) because if they enjoy their job, they will usually take pride in doing it well. I find that enjoyment and motivation often go hand in hand, but as mentioned before, not everyone's motivation is the same, or easily apparent. It is thus important to find and understand what each of your team members is motivated by.

Different Motivations

In practice, understanding what motivates another person cannot always be as easy as just asking them what they enjoy most about their job. For one thing, many people do not even know the answer themselves, in which case you need to help them realise it – something I have had to do on numerous occasions. How do I go about this? I like to praise someone when they succeed, and ask what does that success feels like? The answer is (hopefully!) positive, so I emphasise how they can have those feelings more often if they continue working in the same manner, and also assure them that the longer they keep working to that higher standard, the easier the job will become.

Of course, there will always be people who are mostly or entirely motivated by money – but people tend to shy away from admitting that. If I suspected that that was my teammate's sole or prime motivator, I would always call them out on that by asking outright, is the money you are making important to you? If the answer is yes, then the angle you take is to emphasise that if they continue to succeed, the opportunity to earn more will also rise. It is also important to note that throughout an individual's career, their life circumstances, and their motivations may well change. Personally, when I was just starting my career, I was motivated by career opportunities, and by proving to my family and myself that I could build a successful career. As I proved that this was possible, I began to be more motivated by the potential of higher earnings as the key to buying a property that could one day provide security. So, those conversations about motivation must take place periodically, not just once upon first meeting your team, to ensure you and your team members are still on the same page. For generation Z and Millennials making positive impact in the world, has also become one of the deciding factors in career choices they make. Making positive impact is often closely aligned with people's feeling of purpose; which contributes greatly to their motivation; Every company can help showcase how they make a positive impact by their contribution to GDP, to their workers' welfare and of course if they are making products that are green or have sustainable operations-sharing and socialising company's mission, philanthropic activities within any firm can help tie in purpose with people's motivations. In addition to high earnings potential, steep learning curves, skill acquisition, making world a better place, post pandemic employers also seek for a well-balanced life style that affords people to spend time with their families. Enhancing company policies to ensure that employers get a chance to see their kids off to school once in a while, or take a lunch break to care for their parent is going to help motivate their employers. I would also stress, even if a company policy is not yet well defined, managers should take it on themselves to offer under their discretion the needed flexibility to their team, in doing so retaining and attracting top talent. In the end, it should not always matter when work is done, as long as it is complete at a high standard. To summarise on this topic, understanding people's motivations is indeed very important, I may not be covering all possible motivators, but simply asking someone on a regular basis what it is that drives them, what makes them happy and what motivates them – helps you as a manager to understand how to get the person more effective and how to retain their talent.

The Performance Review

Evaluating a team at the end of the year is something that every manager comes across. During that process, you start remembering all the achievements and mishaps of an individual's performance over the last 12 months. You may be doing that so that you can assign the right level of bonus and adjusted salary for the job that they have done so far – but also this is a great opportunity to assess the potential upside or areas of improvement needed that they may shape their next year. This conversation is also very much linked to that individual's motivation. Going into that conversation your team members should already have a good understanding of where they stand and how the year has gone for them, without any unpleasant surprises. To ensure that, you as a manager need to have been catching up with that person about their performance throughout the year, talking about what they should be doing more of or less of. Your team members will appreciate knowing where they stand which in itself is a great motivator.

Evaluating performance can be done many ways, some companies plot performance of a large organisation on a bell curve to create a normal distribution. This tends to break down as follows: 7% of individuals who can be considered the stars of the team, 20% that do a distinguished job, 40% – the majority of the team – do a good job, then 20% who do a mediocre job and a remainder who need improvement. If you manage with this in mind, then it follows that on a relative basis there will always be someone on your team that needs to do a better job to match their peers. Controversially however if you start off knowing that this is the bell curve that your reps will fit into, at the end of the year, then you don't want (can't afford) each performing as if they were a star. Statistically, this makes sense, unless you are lucky enough to work with an acknowledged elite team that management is happy to subsidise (infamously this was the style of management that Steve Jobs adhered to, hiring just the A-team) and thus you can pay each individual a market value salary increase each year. Also, as a manager, we are encouraged to spend the majority of our time getting more out of top performers or middle-level performers; thus, managing someone like Darren could be beneficial to you, as he would require minimal supervision leaving you with more time managing those stars. This is closely linked to one of the considerations managers have when building a team; too many ambitious high achievers in one team who want your job may be challenging, particularly when you know that only one or two people can reach your level or take over your job when you move on. Thus, having more stars on your team may mean a longer wait for some of those individuals before they have a chance of a promotion in your team – this could lead to losing good people you'd like to retain, who enjoy working with you but feel like they have to move elsewhere to get on. All these considerations will be explored in-depth in Chapters 4 and 5 when we look at building, developing, and retaining your team.

3 – What It Takes
to Build a Strong Team

In other chapters, I have asserted that any manager is only as strong as their weakest teammate. This is not just a clichéd mantra that people say for the sake of saying it; one weak player can genuinely hurt the overall performance, and even the morale, of the whole team. Having a weak link on the team adds an extra burden for you as a manager to carry – it means less time to monitor, mentor, and train the rest of the team, not to mention the drain on your own working time. All this must negatively impact the performance of your whole group. What's more, if your management happens to do a random quality check on your whole team's work or skill levels, they will undoubtedly notice some substandard piece of work or poor practice from that weaker team member. It is crucial that when this observation is made, the poor performer has already been flagged to management by you as needing help and improvement, for which you already have a plan of action in place that you can point to, instead of your bosses discovering this issue on their own. When the problem is finally discovered, by random audit or otherwise, it is much worse if it takes the form of your managers pointing out something that, as far as they can tell, you have missed. This can be seen as a lack of attention to detail if they think you haven't noticed the sub-par performance, and it could be even worse if they think you were aware of the performance but lack the judgement to know it was not good enough – this will cast doubt over your historical performance and that of other teammates. Any of these scenarios will hardly show you in a good light. So how can we avoid these situations, to begin with?

Every manager should come to think of their team as if it is their own business and their own money that is used to hire their people. With this mind-set, you will soon stop accepting or overlooking mediocre performance. Just like a football coach, you want the attacker to be good at scoring and defence to excel at protecting their goal. Similarly, in any team you need to assign the right people to the right tasks – this way, they have every chance, not just to perform adequately, but to excel, maybe even better than you could yourself. If you were going all out to compete against other teams, are your teammates the people you would want on your team? If you have someone on your team that you wouldn't choose in that scenario, then you need to either help them improve their performance or manage them out of your team. This is crucial, as it is a real test of your assessments and your judgement. Everyone deserves the chance to improve and meet expectations, and the potential rewards are well worth the investment of your time. After 1-3 months of assessment, guidance, and feedback, you would hope to see examples of the worker taking feedback on board well and showing concrete signs of improvement. If they do improve at a good rate, fantastic. If they are slow in improving after this time but there are some positive signs, you need to determine if sufficient improvement is possible. There are some people, however, who just do not take well to critical feedback even when it's constructive – this attitude, and the refusal to see a need to change, makes development extremely difficult, if not impossible. In such cases, these people are not a good fit, and probably the job itself is not a good fit for them either, so in the long run, a parting of the ways is mutually beneficial. With experience, your judgement on these calls will get better. In my opinion, until you are nailing these decisions year after year, this is the one area that your manager can always flag as an area for further improvement. Apart from making your judgment look shaky, the harsh fact remains that there is always the chance that a low performer could let you down at the most crucial times when you least expect it. This risk will always loom over you until you resolve it.

Trust

This all comes back to the most important characteristic that you want to have in your people: trust. Trust can be portrayed in many ways, and here I'll look at the 'Send and Forget' concept. This is when you can delegate a task onto someone and have complete faith, not only that the task will be done promptly without you chasing, but it will be completed to a high standard. So complete is this faith that you wouldn't even need to check as you know that person will have done a great job. These people are not easy to come by, and typically this is someone you have worked with before. Someone you have gone through some ups and downs with and learned through adversity that you have each other's backs and have confidence that even if they don't yet have all the relevant expertise for the new role, they will seek your help or find someone else to help them get the job done as needed. It is no wonder that you see managers bring people like this with them to job after job and assign them to high-level positions. They trust these people implicitly after working and succeeding with them before. As noted in Chapter 1, your management style may differ greatly depending on whether you are managing a team of individuals that you already know and trust, or a new team that you are still getting to know (and vice versa). With a team of known, trusted individuals, your style of management will lean towards delegation and less micromanagement.

With a more junior or unfamiliar team, you need to spend time asserting yourself and setting out what you want, as well as gauging their quality. The process of getting to know your new teammates will by definition involve a lot of speaking to them, and continuous scrutiny of their work (both the end product, and their methods). This may well be perceived as invasive micromanagement, particularly if the staff are long-serving in their roles and/or the company. That said, experienced workers should expect and accept that any newly appointed manager will take a closer look at their work, and ask more questions, during the transitional period. The issue of course is how these questions are asked, and the level of disruption new management brings to the team during the transition period. If you are a new manager, then it is best to have coaching around this with HR as early as possible, to ensure you do not rub people the wrong way. It is important not to underestimate that this is a tough period for all parties, and the key to managing it successfully is to keep disruption to a minimum. This is easier said than done, as many people use this opportunity to rebel, and to spend time gossiping and complaining about the change instead of looking for the positives. During this period, you can get to see who your stars are, and who stands out negatively for their lack of enthusiasm. Over my managerial career, I have been the new girl on the block, coming in to manage a hitherto unknown sales team, but also have run teams containing some people I had a prior relationship with. Those relationships can be helpful when gauging the mood of the group and getting insight into the background behind some situations which can help with getting ahead of potential trouble spots. To my detriment, I always felt that I could not rely on just one person's perspective and was determined to uncover or check a lot of details by myself, either to make certain or seek a wider opinion from others. I found out the hard way that if you ask someone a question, and then choose to double-check the answer you get, then they can feel are not being trusted, which can have the opposite to your intended trust-building effect. If that happens to you, don't be afraid to go back to that person, apologise for any offence and clear the air. Explain that you are getting to know a lot of new people and exploring how they are feeling about the evolving new situation. As a manager, you are building consensus as well as understanding who is integral to your plans for the group. To head off gossip or dissatisfaction, it is crucial to always be transparent in your communication and not hide behind 'he said she said' – if misunderstandings happen, just speak to people directly. After you have been managing the team for a while, the need for this scrutiny should die down, and people on the team will feel less under the microscope. By then, they will also know your expectations (if they don't, then something is wrong!). It is no wonder that after any manager has been in the same role for two years or more, their management style changes to less micro and more trusting. Having trusted members on the team, even if it's as few as, say, 3 out of 10 teammates, not only helps managers delegate but frees up their focus to help them and the team excel in other areas of business. If you are new on the managerial ladder, then you can start building that cohort who in the future you can trust to do a good job and earmark to bring with you into other roles. There are many techniques for gaining someone's trust – believing in them, and making them feel appreciated, are both powerful motivators. If you believe in your people, reward them, provide them with additional responsibilities and promotions, they will feel gratitude and, in my experience, do not forget the manager that promoted them. Not necessarily because you praised them or tried to win them over – but also if you challenged them to improve or support them in career struggles. If you had someone's back in a dispute, an individual would appreciate that (and if they don't, I suggest you don't want them following you!). If you were able to reward someone for their effort at the end of the year this will go a long way. If you recognise their achievements, not only do you raise your peoples' visibility across the firm, but you are also opening potential exciting future opportunities for them. Once your management knows about people you value, and why, it also becomes that extra bit easier for you to fight for their enhanced end-of-year compensation, and helping your people get paid also wins you their trust and appreciation.

If you spend some time with your team outside the office and actually get to know each other and share life stories, this will also help build a bridge of trust, similar to what you do when you first meet anyone and create friendships in the outside world. Introducing a level of comradery on your team helps you build trust with your team members and is also part of a healthy environment.

All these are practical examples of how to cultivate a team of people who follow you and trust you, and who you can trust in return. This of course is not a perfect formula, and when you trust someone, they don't by default start trusting you back. Over time, though, you do earn people's trust, and your actions can help you to do that quicker.

Understanding People's Motivations and Skillsets

If you are starting anew and do not yet have that group of trusted individuals to bring on board, worry not – you will build them. With time, people will buy into your strengths, and you will build up an army of followers. It doesn't happen overnight of course; you need to prove that you have people's back, that you are credible, you can and do advance other people's careers and make them better at what they do. This goes hand in hand with understanding other people's strengths. If you understand what everyone on the team is good at and what some of their drawbacks are, you should focus on their strengths.

Focusing on someone's strength helps them to feel good about themselves. People like doing what they are good at, and the more they do it the more valued they feel. A happy employee will get you results that an unhappy worker wouldn't. Someone who is happy will also make the working environment and atmosphere much better which will help attract more talent into your team. It is also important to align their strength with the right strategy. Someone's strength could be market or product-specific; it could be their soft skills of selling or servicing clients, it could be technical know-how, or being a good people person who could one day make a good leader themselves. The job of a good manager is to get each person doing more of what they are good at; if someone is good at selling, they should not be spending 80% of their time on account management. If a person is more technical and doesn't like client interactions, don't try, and force them into client-facing duties – people can learn to cover up their weaknesses, and even gain a degree of competence, but they won't show any flair in these uncomfortable roles, and you'll never get those benefits we just covered.

The biggest lesson I have learned: in my experience, you can't teach someone to be inquisitive by nature, to be driven by a hunger for results. People either have it or they don't; it is part of their character. The time you spend trying to change someone's character is time wasted. Time is the only aspect you can control so do you want to spend your time trying to change someone, with no guarantee it will work, or do you spend time getting someone to do what you already know they are good at? The latter will get you better results. Managers tend to spend most of their time either with poor performers, trying to transform them into superstars, or good performers trying to get more out of them. I challenge managers to flip that and start spending most of their time on getting their superstars to perform at an exceptional level and raising the bar higher for the other good performers on the team. The poor performers will very quickly recognise their drawbacks, and you may be surprised to see how many of them will either voluntarily seek to get help or will ask to move to do something else. Throughout my career, I have been able to succeed by learning on the job, as well as listening to senior managers who offered their wisdom. Above all, there is a difference between being taught to do something and learning by yourself by experience. The more experience you gain, the better you become. Trial and error and multiple repetitions in my opinion is a winning recipe. As you do something many times over, you will encounter problems and scenarios that no one can prepare you for. With experience, your reactions to different scenarios, your responses to people, become more polished until you can react in a way that resolves any tricky situation quickly without minimal fallout. For an individual contributor, this takes the form of making calls, writing notes, or running training. As a manager, it is essential to confirm the quality needed for these tasks so that when you see that an area needs to be worked on, you can articulate quickly and clearly what a good standard of work looks like. Then you can get that person doing the same task over and over to the desired quality level. The more they do it, the better they get, the easier the tasks get, the quicker they can complete them. Once they have mastered doing these quickly and well, it will leave them with more time to work on picking up valuable skills or completing other projects. In theory, this all sounds perfect. Get people to become great at what they do, they will realise they are good at it and hence will earn and enjoy praise for it. However, in practice, it is of course never that simple. A person's daily agenda never just consists of tackling one task which they are good at. There will be other mundane day-to-day operational processes to carry out. Putting processes in place, leveraging technology, and delegating certain tasks out to either hungry juniors or even other departments, may be the answer here; but you also need to have people on your team that can get the job done. They are on the same page as you and understand the importance of mastering the basics before moving on to tackle other creative and innovative areas of business.

The Hiring Process

So, how do you ensure that you hire people that you know will listen to feedback, be goal-oriented, and constructively voice their opinions without always having to disagree with organisational vision. Those people will most likely have the desire to succeed and be ambitious to advance their careers. In my experience, the job of selecting a good team is half done once you have identified people who are a good cultural fit for the company. Those individuals are very much aligned with the company vision, hungry for success, and willing to get their hands dirty to get results. This can be spotted in an interview, by spending more time finding out about individuals' previous experience, the results they achieved, and how. Hiring is, therefore, one of the most important tasks that a manager can and should undertake. In some organisations, it is customary to have the potential employee meet with the team and be interviewed by them, which gets you more information on them and is a great test of whether that individual would be a good fit with the team. Teamwork and creating a good, happy team spirit are essential for achieving every manager's end goals. By getting more opinions on the person you are looking to hire, you also share ownership of making the hire work well with everyone who advocated for that candidate. One of the interview red flags that always grabs my attention is when a person is not prepared. It sounds so simple, but it is surprising to see how many people come through the door of an interview without having done their due diligence. The minimum preparation should be understanding what they are applying for; they must know what your company does or makes and who the competition is. They should also have good answers as to why they want to join your company, and their skillset must fit the job description they are applying for. Their skills should ideally be backed up by previous professional or educational experience. When prodded for further examples of their experience and achievements, those need to be articulated well, with any unfamiliar concepts explained clearly and promptly. This will also test their communication skills. I typically also ask about their previous working relationships, the rapport they had with previous managers. I ask if there have ever been disagreements and if so, how they handled it. It is essential to focus on at least one professional example in detail, to get a sense of a person's true characteristics and persons cultural attributes. I always want to leave an interview with an opinion about someone, or a fact that has personally intrigued my interest and left an impression. One lesson I have learned is to listen to my gut feeling. If after an interview I am not 100% sure, if I find myself worrying about the candidate possibly being a poor fit, it is usually because they would be. If you need to spend significant time contemplating whether it is a yes or a no, it should mean no rather than yes. You want to pick people who stand out as a clear yes, even if this means restarting the hiring process. That may be costly and time-consuming (and no doubt will not endear you to HR colleagues). But it is also costly to hire and train a new hire, only to find out that after your all investment on that person, you lose them to competition or other companies, or that they simply can't or won't do the job you've hired them for – if things get to that point, you will soon be looking for a replacement again anyway. If I see that the candidate is a good fit, I tend to also spend some time outlining potential drawbacks of the role they are applying for, as it's also important that the candidate can see if the job is the right fit for them. An interview needs to be a two-way process for candidates to see if this is the right opportunity for them as much as it is for the employer. This way you ensure that it is not an exercise in wasted time with potentially costly repercussions.

Building the Diverse Team

Diversity and inclusion are not just hot topics to pay lip service to or tick a box. It is morally right to make any workplace inclusive and not tolerate any discrimination. What's more, if companies don't put this near the top of their internal priorities, many if not all external clients will simply walk away from them – I have seen many business relationships go sour and even end, after one party is called out on discrimination. Diversity and inclusivity should also be key organisational goals for practical reasons, as they are vital ingredients in a successful business. Having a diverse pool of candidates applying for (and filling) roles at your company is the only way to achieve a diverse way of thinking. Very often a manager tends to hire mini versions of themselves. This inclination is understandable; after all, if you are a manager it's because you were able to rise through the ranks and build a successful career, so of course you want people with the same drive and skills as yourself to join the team. The trouble with that, however, is you are trying to create more managers like you, but that's not what a team needs to be built of (plus only one or maybe two of them would have any realistic chance at your or similar management roles any time soon). What you need to round out the team is specialists or salespeople or relationship managers.

Beyond considerations of career progression and team balance, trying to replicate yourself will just duplicate your thinking, their ideas will also be similar to yours and one another, and the client type they can relate to and work well with will also be limited. Another good reason why diversity of a team is crucial in any global organisation is that you have more chance to build strong relationships with foreign clients if you have staff in your team with similar life experiences and backgrounds (national, cultural, or linguistic), either to liaise with them directly or offer insights to the teammate covering that account. People open up more and relate quicker to people with similar backgrounds as them. For major international companies, you may end up with a wide range of cultural, ethnic, and national backgrounds. Each person brings a unique perspective, which can be extremely helpful particularly when solving complex issues or devising unique strategies when you want to outshine your competition.

In my experience with European teams, you will most likely need some or all of your team to have certain language skills. That does, of course, add extra complexity to your hiring needs, so it is thus incredibly important to always maintain a pipeline of people that you are suitable for your group. In today's fast-paced global work environment, people with language skills have extra options to move on, and hence you need to have your plan B and succession planning ready.

Another tip I have learned is that not all jobs in a travelling team need to have language needs, globalisation works in your favour, particularly in the main financial hubs. Hence when building a team to cover, say, Germany, it may be useful for your diversity of different cultures to not just have German nationals covering it. As a manager, you can hire an English or Dutch speaker to cover that region too – due to globalisation many people do speak English in these countries and there will also be, for instance, a significant Dutch community there too.

Helena Morrissey's 2018 book *A Good Time to Be a Girl*[2] offers a great example outlining why companies should keep a diversity of candidate outlook at the forefront of their mind. Let's say we have candidate A and candidate B in for an interview, which includes a round of test questions. Candidate A answers 8/10 questions correctly and candidate B gets 4/10. At first glance, it seems obvious to pick candidate A. However, what if you learn that the questions that candidate B got right are the ones candidate A got wrong and that those same questions were answered wrong by 90% of all other candidates and current team members. The different thinking of candidate B will be able to fill the gap in the firm and get better results all around. As a manager, your goal is to solve as many problems as possible that come your way, to produce

---

[2] https://www.harpercollins.co.uk/9780008241643/a-good-time-to-be-a-girl/

strong strategic initiatives and be able to execute on them. If everyone thinks the same way, you miss those interesting ideas and you miss the ability to be challenged and learn from each other. Throughout my career, I have had feedback that because of the high standards I set for myself and my managers, they were forced to up their game and became better managers as a result. Having a colleague who shows a different mindset and who questions established practices can be tricky to adapt to at first, yet it pays off in the long run. Having a high performer on the team who thinks differently than you will keep you busy and on your toes; will do more to challenge your assumptions and improve your management style than any number of mini-me manager clones. As a manager, you cannot afford to become complacent and think you know it all, and an injection of high performers with unfamiliar mindsets and backgrounds will prevent that complacency. Diversity in your team is not simply a matter of hiring a wide range of ethnicities, ages, and genders, but also hiring external candidates instead of looking in the house – people who can bring wider and different market knowledge to your team. I covered this before in Chapter 2's section on *Managing entrenched long-serving colleagues,* but it's also worth considering that people with outside experience may be more senior not only in experience but age, and it is important as a manager to be humble when managing these individuals. Managing experienced senior employers can be a breath of fresh air. Many times, such people are mature, they react appropriately to orders, and can suggest various valid ways in which things can be approached – they just get it. They can be an extremely useful source of insight and suggestions for handling market issues and trends, and of course, they are likely to bring in well-established connections.

It's not just these established team players who can be a useful resource for you, of course. Take comfort in the fact that as a manager, you need not always be the best at everything. Appreciate that you have people on the team who will support you where you may have knowledge gaps. This doesn't expose you as a weak manager – on the contrary, while good managers should be strong generalists in all areas, they should also be secure enough to admit when they need help and know who to turn to when things get more specific. You shouldn't feel threatened by these incoming specialists – remember, you possess the relationships and internal network knowledge, that differentiates you from any external hire, and you also hold leadership skills that have put you where you are. Bringing a talented, diverse team together and being able to retain them is a key metric of a successful manager.

One challenge that you as manager of this diverse team may face is the different communication styles that different types of people have. To overcome this, you need to create good synergies – not always an easy task. I have had managers who just clashed with certain individuals on their team, due to their different styles and mindsets. I always encourage that manager to perform the following exercise: what are the four strengths that this person has? What benefits do those attributes bring to the team? Every individual has such strengths, so a manager helps themselves by selling these advantages to himself first, and then it is a question of aligning that person with the right task and the right group of colleagues/clients. Once everyone is set, in the right team doing the right job, you then can choose the right management style that works best for your team which helps you gain results, retain, and motivate people; and this of course is key to any team's success.

4 – How to Successfully Retain People

Could any manager succeed without a team that executes on a strategy and reaches its yearly targets? We all know the answer to that, so after recruiting your dream team, the next challenge then facing you is retaining them. Recruiting talent is costly, that should not be underestimated, but if you then lose a good individual the cost doubles. Not only do you need to find a suitable replacement, but you may also pay a high time cost in doing so if your succession planning isn't already in place. Time is a commodity you have to optimise, and if you do not have the right person in place or lined up for the right role, you pay a high opportunity cost, allowing your competitors to snatch up the best talent. There will always be personnel movement; people do move on to take up other challenges and to advance their careers. It is therefore crucial that you always have backup plans and a healthy pipeline of good candidates who have the potential to help your team. Joining a successful team with high performers is highly motivating, thus maintaining a strong team by retaining your best talent in the first place is doubly advantageous to you as a manager.

How do you ensure you retain talent? Understanding the motivations of each individual is of course the first step, but not the whole solution. Your style of management and your ability to adjust your tone and management approach to different people is crucial as well. There is a saying, 'people don't leave companies, they leave their managers'. There is some truth to this, since if you still feel motivated and inspired by your managers, and if you are constantly learning from them, then the chances of you wanting to move on will be much slimmer.

People management is an art form that managers get better at with experience, but the cost of inexperience can often be high – as high as the resignation of a talented employee. This has a financial impact of course, due to the loss of their performance and the cost of finding and training their replacement. There is also the reputational risk if this disenchanted employee goes on to share their poor experience in the wider marketplace. Depending on the field and location you work in, there may be a surprisingly small labour pool, and word travels far and fast about the good or bad experiences people have had in past roles. There is also a potential personal cost, as a manager who loses talent on regular basis will find their management style under scrutiny be assessed. The goal of this chapter is to help you speed up the learning process without paying a high cost of learning from fatal mistakes.

Setting the Tone

As a manager, you need to create a positive atmosphere so that everyone in your team feels appreciated and valued.

The aim is to get people on your side, get them to buy into your strategic goals, and want to work collectively in reaching it. In a good environment like this, your people look forward to coming to work and collaborating. If the environment you as a manager set is not positive, then it will be hard to retain any individual.

In terms of my tips for setting the tone, I have made the same interesting observation repeatedly over the years – and that is how differently people act outside of work to the way they do with their colleagues. It always baffles me. For instance, I see colleagues being reasonable, polite, and considerate in their approach when dealing with, say, serving staff at a restaurant, or the airport check-in desk, even amidst a stressful situation like a ruined meal or a delayed flight. However, I then see those same calm, understanding individuals turn into demanding, impatient authoritarian tyrants when they are wearing their manager hats at work. Why this inconsistency? As a customer they are polite when receiving a service, yet when they are supposed to be coaching others to provide a service to their end customers or internal stakeholders they take a very different approach, not realising that their team members will internalise and mimic some of this negative behaviour they have themselves been victims of. Managers should never forget it is their core human self, not just their professional skillset, which has gotten them promoted. It is their manner and behaviour which govern the way other people respond to them and will win people over or drive them away. It is a cliché but speak to others as you'd like to be spoken to yourself. As mentioned previously, people typically do not leave the company, they leave their managers. If you are a nice person who gets on with your team members, even if you are not so talented as a manager you will usually find that your team will want to work for you and give you time and feedback to improve. Therefore, first and foremost an important aspect of retaining talent is to be nice, fair, and have time for your people. If as a person you are upbeat, professional, and always work with other people politely, then your job as a manager will be already off to an easier start.

Managing Different Personalities

Different personalities require different styles of management. Half the manager's job is done once you understand the other person's style and what type of management they best respond to. Most managers already know to manage a high performer differently from the way they would manage a struggling performer, but furthermore, you should also manage an ambitious and developing high performer differently from a high performer who has reached their full potential. Let's look at the first case, the ambitious, still-growing high performer. You would reward them with projects and responsibilities that will help them stay competitive and provide a platform for them to shine. You most likely will not micromanage these individuals and use a delegation approach instead. You should also ensure to maintain positive upbeat interactions with this person. It is also important not to forget that today's high performer may not have such a good year next year, but the underlying motivations of any one person will unlikely to change much unless they are volatile individuals; by staying close to your people, you will be able to read them and adjust your approach if needed. A high performer who has reached their full potential does need variety so that they still feel challenged. Make sure they are frequently exposed to different experiences and new sets of people to influence and be influenced by thus expanding their network. Different experiences will also activate someone's seeking mechanism to question, learn and develop new skills; as Daniel Cable cites in his book *Alive at work*, not only does that bring renewed energy, creativity but also releases dopamine which increases employer's motivation.

On the other side of the spectrum, if you have an average performer who is happy doing what they are doing without putting in extra effort, your approach would be to set their projects with clear deadlines, regular check-ups, and a keep a close managerial watch. There should never be a question of you favouring one performer over the other, so communication should stay consistent, but the amount of time you spend with them and how many ongoing projects you delegate to them will vary due to performance and experience.

There are many factors in determining what type of individual you are dealing with; for instance, is this an ambitious, competitive individual, or a cautious analytical type? An enthusiastic people person or a thoughtful introvert. It's good to remember that someone can be all these things at once. However, one or two traits are usually their dominant leading ones. There are a thousand personality tests out there promising to identify your personality type and how your personality reacts to a stressful environment. One that I have found particularly useful is the Insights Discovery [3]approach.

---

[3] https://www.insights.com/products/insights-discovery/

This theory divides people into four main personality groups, as decided by question answers and behaviour insights, which are represented by four colours: red, blue, yellow, and green. People who express a consistent set of characteristics are naturally felt inclined to react to certain situations with similar communication styles. So, as a manager, knowing what type of people you have on your team and what 'colour' of communication technique would be more effectively received by that individual could help create harmonious relationships between manager and team member. For instance, a person who is classified red (typically highly competitive, ambitious, natural leader types), would respond better when you are concise, quick, and to the point. Yellow (Enthusiasts) people are eager and keen networkers, and an effective communication approach with these individuals involves giving them the big picture to start with plus lots of information. Green (Amiable) staff are centred on relationships and people, who want to see how anything would impact their team and/or clients. These sociable people need to be shown that you care and that you are empathetic. Finally, blue represents analytical people, who cherish detail and data and are the most patient of all in terms of carefully forming their strategy using all available information before acting.

Communication Style

By communication skills, I mainly refer here to the approach you take to reach each individual. How you balance the independence and guidance you provide to your team; how much you get involved and how much you leave to your team to forge ahead; you can only make these judgements once you spend some time with your people and get to know them. This can be deduced best by simply asking your direct reports; what would you like to receive from me during your one-to-ones? Would you appreciate more hands-on input, or do you operate better when left to your own devices? Of course, if they say they want a more independent approach, but you note that there are recurring issues, you need to feed that back and let them know that you believe that more hands-on mentoring from you will accelerate their development. I have often been surprised in the past by how many of my direct reports have asked me to be more hands-on, wanting to be guided and to introduce regular catch-ups to assess progress and also to share their achievements and challenges. By asking them what type of management they needed from me, I provided them with a choice. Many of my staff appreciated this consultation, feeling that I was trusting them and treating them as capable adults by letting them decide how to be managed.

Whatever communication approach you take with an individual needs to be tailored and constantly evolving. A performer can feel demotivated if the wrong communication style is applied. As with most management, with experience, you will get better at this, and my suggestion is to have an external expert coach go over different approaches you may take, and have the team discuss different communication styles in a group with them. Talking this through helps you think about it and then put it into practice. It is especially helpful to have such an external consultant run the workshops and ascertaining the best plan of action or best communication style if you have been dealing with a negative relationship situation for a while and need a different perspective. I cannot stress enough how far a good management performance is intertwined with that ability to connect with people through the appropriate communication skills.

Managing the Struggling Performer

After spending time with each individual, you should soon identify the weaker links on the team. Spotting and addressing weak performance is important beyond its impact on the team's numbers. Of course, the poor performer is likely to be stressed and miserable. Being good at something is phenomenal, as you reach your goals and have your achievements rewarded and celebrated. But the opposite is also brutally true when things are not going well enough despite your best efforts. Nor is the damage limited to that one struggling individual, because, as mentioned before, people are motivated not only by their managers but by the people and atmosphere they work with. Other teammates get demotivated when they see someone not pulling their weight, and it is also distressing to see a colleague having a hard time and being miserable. They will look to you to fix the situation. It is crucial to ask what is making this person a weaker performer. Is it an under-developed skill, such as specific technical knowledge, is it their style of communication, or a lack of hunger to perform and develop? Does the individual actually understand what is expected of them? It may be the case that expectations have changed over time, or they were not initially communicated clearly. Especially if you are a new manager, it is always useful to start from basics and hold those conversations early on so that everyone knows what is expected. Similarly, if you have been in a role for some time, but the person changed responsibilities within their role, it is again crucial to touch base to reset expectations and confirm priorities.

Setting clear expectations and ensuring that all relevant training has been done is crucial before you can fairly ascertain whether this person is a poor performer. Managers should not forget that above all they are coaches, and that coaching should not just be limited to technical knowledge. The tasks you set your team need to be clearly defined and to some extend accompanied with instructions on how to perform them well if you want a guaranteed level of performance quality. Without going through each task, you set, you take it for granted that your people know what they are meant to be doing or providing. This may not be the case, especially if your procedures or workflows are complex, or someone has done a rushed job of briefing them. In such a case, it could well be that it was your expectations, not their performance, that was unreasonable; a situation which will cause problems and stress for all the team.

If, however, your expectations have been clear and reasonable all along, the right training has taken place and the person's performance is still below expectations, then more thought is needed. You can approach this in a few ways. Perhaps you have seen enough positive aspects that, in your opinion, you still could coach them up. You can create a short-term plan of action, with tangible goals that the individual needs to meet weekly. Once you see the improvement you can congratulate the individual and move them onto more complex tasks and repeat the process of evaluation and workload escalation until you see sustained real improvement in their results and approach. Perhaps this person possesses different, currently underutilised strengths which you could still draw on, and better leverage their talents by shifting them into a new role within your team. You may think there is a better fit for their strengths and skills in another department where they will more likely succeed. This is a tough sell, however, as other managers may perceive it as you just passing on your problem and be reluctant to give your castoff a chance. It can also reflect badly on your judgement if a managerial colleague *does* take a chance on redeeming that person's potential only to get the same poor results, so you need to be confident before going down this route. As mentioned, all of these options would be far cheaper than having to go through a brand-new hiring process, not to mention being a positive and rewarding management success for you, and of course a much better resolution for the employee in question!

The last route is that you performance-manage them towards an exit via formal written warnings and ultimately termination. Unfortunately, in my experience, this is never a pleasant experience for anyone involved. However, it is rewarding for many people once it is done, as it is only this way that they can ultimately progress into a career and a role where they are happy and indeed make a better fit. Thus, once the person sees clearly that there are flaws in their performance which they cannot fix despite all the opportunities offered by your performance intervention, they almost always accept the fact of it and move on. At the end of the day, there are always other jobs and avenues out there where they can reinvent themselves more fruitfully. In practice, the process of managing someone out is very time intensive and can be frustrating as well as distracting you from more profitable work with high performers and considering your overall business strategy. Nevertheless, it needs doing – until it's dealt with, that is a headcount that is occupied by someone not performing and filling it with someone good will bring you better results overall. No matter what level of a performer you are managing, your management style needs to be respectful, even-tempered, positive, and approachable to all. These are all human beings who deserve your respect, no matter what their performance is like. You may say "Of course they are – this is simply common sense so why are you bothering to make a point of this?" I make it because I have seen managers walk straight past their poorer performers and not acknowledge their existence in front of their peers. If there is any chance for turning this person's performance around, this type of management is not it. I have managed someone out in the past, and they left on positive terms because we agreed that this was not the best fit for that person's skillset. It was professional and civil throughout. I also managed someone else who was put on a performance plan – I discovered that the expectations set were not clear, they were not organised, and were drowning in administrative tasks instead of focusing on what mattered for the business. This experience was not a positive one at the time, but this person took all the directions provided, changed their priorities, and persevered. This experience was hugely positive in the end – not only did this person improve his way out of the performance plan, but he also then continued to excel until three years later he was promoted to manager of that team. I love that example because it shows how dramatically a person's performance can be changed if you manage them the right way during tough times. The company has now ended up with a motivated, content, and skilled individual. I now have a high-achieving mentee who feels grateful that I dedicated so much time to salvaging their performance. He appreciated my investment in him and has stayed loyal to me throughout his career. A big ingredient in this success story is the communication style I chose when managing this individual, a consultative approach with clearly laid out reasoning for each key element of the job he was struggling with. If I had chosen to use a different tone in our performance management meetings with this individual if I had been visibly frustrated and not giving that person the time to justify my commitment to their progress, this may not have had such a happy ending.

The One-to-One Meeting

Your communication skills as a manager are mostly practised and tested during your one-to-ones with your team. One-to-ones with direct reports are my most important meetings during the week, just as their end-of-year reviews are the most important meetings of the last 12 months. Why? This is the time your employees value the most when they get to talk to you about their achievements, about how they are doing, and any issues they may have. As Dale Carnegie's famous book *How to win friends and Influence People* states, lesson number one is to let people speak. Everyone likes talking about themselves. Your one-to-ones with your people should always have a personal touch. Not just because you will most likely spend more time with these individuals than you do at home with your family, but also because by speaking to people about their personal lives you remove a potential hurdle for first managers; it breaks the ice and puts people at ease. People want to work for people they can learn from relating to, not someone they get an impersonal grilling from. As this is the most important time during your week, coming prepared is crucial. The one-to-one is your teammate's time with you, thus most likely they should be the ones driving the agenda. However, you too should have two or three points ready to discuss (more on the importance of this shortly). By having a structured agenda, you will make this time more valuable for them if they aren't prepared or willing to start. The key is to listen, take good notes, and have clear follow-up items that you can return to in the next meeting. Your goals are aligned; the successful performance of your team member is what you both want. It's important therefore to touch base on progress towards targets, and how they feel you can help them achieve those. What are the current business drivers they need to consider and are they facing any hurdles to hitting targets or career progress obstacles that you can help resolve? You will most likely spend some time talking about other stakeholders that influence the target, are they getting what they need from individuals, and is everyone pulling their weight. Your meeting is also a forum to broach any analysis or upper management updates that they may find useful.

Feedback on performance and career progression is something your direct reports will be looking for from you; my direct reports always appreciate how, if they ask for feedback, I have prepared two or three examples where I have been impressed and one or two areas where I feel more work can still be done. This is something you will get from your repeated interactions with one another –no one is perfect, and it is your job to identify a few areas where you can help improve your team member's performance. Once I asked my manager how he thought I was doing, and he replied that he wanted to collate his thoughts and come back to me. I immediately realised that he didn't have examples to hand, and that made me feel a little unsure of my performance – would he come back with negative or positive feedback? Most of all, I wondered what was stopping him from just sharing one or two examples where I exceeded expectations or where he felt there was room to further improve. I had to wonder how much he cared or paid attention to my career and performance, which didn't help me feel valued or important to the wider team or company landscape. If you are a manager who stays close to your people and wants them to know you are invested in their progress, such examples should always be at your fingertips. To sum up the structure of a successful one-to-one: business (results vs targets), people (effectiveness of stakeholder interactions), upper management direction; strategy for the week, and finally specific feedback. This is the broad template that I adhere to when preparing for one-to-one but just like with everything, nothing is ever set and stone; there may be times when you spend your whole one-to-one on one significant problem or issue or coaching the individual on a particular topic or skill. In the past, I have had managers who felt that because I was experienced and they have managed me for a while, this hour can be shortened or skipped altogether. I disagree. The more valuable interactions you have with your team, the more you get to know about your people's performance and experiences, and the more you can influence a positive outcome. If you are not close to the ins and outs of your team's performance and their daily issues, you may get too far removed from the business, and compromise your ability to influence the end-of-year results. If your team challenges you on the frequency of their one-to-ones, look into the quality of those and what you bring to them. Some managers review the performance of their team and outline what was done well or poorly and any lessons to be learned from it; a retrospective approach. It is always easiest to look back in time and draw conclusions. There is definite value and need for this aspect, in terms of evaluations and lessons for the future. However, I am a bigger fan of proactively preparing the team for the best potential outcome before an activity starts, so that I can better prepare them to succeed. To give an example: before I go to shadow a rep for the first time, it is much more useful that I check their understanding of the meeting goals and help them prepare better beforehand, rather than letting them go in the meeting blind and provide negative feedback after the event about what they could have done better. Now if this is a second shadowing session, it is sensible to use that approach, to shadow how well they can do it this time without your coaching, and then share your thoughts afterwards. Your team member will appreciate your investment of time and effort into their development, which of course is what all managers should aim for. Your one-to-one is a facilitated forum for spending time with your people. Without this, you will not be able to truly know them, their strengths, and weaknesses as well as the state of the business. Above all, it allows you to get to know your people on a personal level, which is also crucially important to building a rapport and trust as well as being able to notice if something is off with them so that you as a manager can support them. All of us have personal lives and at times things get tough; to give you an example, I once noticed that one of my team members was unusually quiet. I didn't want to pry but I did eventually ask "Is everything ok? You seem quiet today" (you could also ask something like "How was your weekend, did you get up to anything fun?" – if the response is silent or a non-committal, "Nothing really, just stayed in", and you know that this person is typically active and chatty, you may want to press some more). Even if they don't give any clear indication of a problem but you still feel that something is off, just make sure that your people know you are there for them; even knowing that can be supportive and helpful.

Empathy

A big part of any manager's soft skills is the ability to listen and be empathetic. Being empathetic means being able to relate to the issues people are experiencing, by first listening to them, asking the right questions to engage in a dialogue, and relating to the situation. Empathy is *not* automatically saying "I know how you feel as it also happened to me once" – that response is making it about you and indicates that you aren't listening to their personal experience. You need to listen to what they are saying as every situation, and how people respond to it, is unique. People want to be heard and you need to hear them speak their minds. You can, of course, relate to what they are going through and offer ideas or potential solutions where that is appropriate or suggest resources to help the person find a solution themselves. No matter how trivial you may think the situation is, you should never just say "everything will be ok, cheer up" – this is hugely patronising and at that particular time the situation requires empathy not trite optimism. If you are unable to find time for your people where you listen and display empathy, you are not fostering an environment of trust. Without nurturing an atmosphere where staff feels that their lives and concerns are valued, it is tough to retain people.

Providing Feedback

Many companies are trending towards standing meetings to reduce the time spent talking rather than working. I agree that many meetings can be shortened or removed altogether. I do still feel that there is always a need to meet with your team members, even if it is to celebrate together what they are proud of from the last fortnight's performance and devise ways to replicate and build on such success; you can use this for promoting this individual and further your understanding of how best to retain them. People always appreciate you sharing their concerns and talking through some potential solutions and offering them your knowledge of resources they may use. One subject matter that comes up in many people's annual feedback sessions is the lack of conversations on career progressions. Truth be told, no one is going to care about your career as much as you do. However, if you are an outstanding manager you will pick up on that subject during your monthly catch-ups. Setting up a clear goal of what is the next career step for your team member, including milestones to reach or skillsets to master. This will demonstrate that you truly are invested in your people's career progression. The development of your people should be part of every retention plan. There are many practical approaches you could consider for investing in your people: creating training courses, establishing mentorship programs, or running manager-coaching sessions. During such coaching sessions, do not underestimate the power of giving effective feedback (a subject intricately linked to communication skills). People should always know where they stand and what they need to work on. There is always room for improvement, even for your top performer. Providing constructive, actionable feedback is crucial, and is much appreciated and highly sought after by individual contributors. How to deliver your feedback is just as important. It needs to be concise, backed by an example or two illustrating how certain behaviour impacted either other people or the business, and what can be learned from each example. Everything should always link back either to the business or the impact that this person's action or inaction has had on other people. Similarly, feedback for poorer performers should ensure that they receive concise, relevant examples tied to their performance every week. Without providing regular feedback, managers are effectively neglecting not only the development pillar of their responsibilities but also the retention pillar; if you spend no time developing people they will not feel you are investing in their career. Managers need to be specific when providing feedback and break it down for the recipient so that they understand the reasons why some of their actions did not have the desired or expected reaction. Let's go through an example of this. When you have an ambitious high-performing person, they are typically involved in projects beyond their role. They want to drive change in the organisation and in so doing have many interactions with different stakeholders of the firm, all of whom are themselves pursuing their agenda. In this example, my high performer has historically been told that the communication style they take in approaching these situations may not be the most appropriate. Now in my opinion that type of feedback is not the most effective. If you start your feedback just saying that their communication style has a negative impact, you will generate a defensive reaction, provoking resistance and possibly resentment; you need to back it up, give an example and explain in detail what exactly that impact was, and how it could be avoided. 'Communication style' is a very broad term and should be broken down and analysed at the level of clear specifics, for instance: "When you positioned the issue only from your angle, in an emotive way, the person you talked to, felt to put on the defensive. It would help immensely if you calmly first gave the context and explained the impact this could have on the business…" Similarly, during your one to one, if you are talking about actions they've taken, and trying to understand their reasoning, make sure you think about how you phrase your questions. Using the word "why" instead of "what" and "how" is likely to provoke a defensive response and reduces your chance of positive learning interaction. Question starting with the word "why" will always cause the receiving party responding from a position of defence, whereas if you start with "what" and "how" this is an open-end question giving the other party an invitation to explain the logic behind their choice of actions. All of this is part of your one-to-one and should take place regularly. If you don't have this in place, and then abruptly provide negative feedback without any positive analysis or constructive advice, then your people will feel that you only see the negative side to their performance.

They will come to dread your catch-ups. Never forget that feedback should focus just as much on the constructive and positive, as well as finding fault and identifying problems. Without recognition and praise, they may feel less motivated which will lower morale on the team; good morale, and an enjoyable atmosphere is crucial for retention. Feedback is an essential weapon in the manager's arsenal for retaining and developing talent; in my experience, giving it consistently and in a measured tone, goes a long way in retaining your top individuals and even transforming mediocre performers into good ones.

On the flip side, managers who only ever just provide positive feedback run the risk of losing trust from their team. I had a manager who only ever said positive, uplifting things, so much so that I felt he was grooming me to eventually get his job. But after I overheard him saying the same things to my peers, right then and there I lost any trust that his feedback was anything more than generic positive fluff that my manager used with everyone to win them over. Such a context-free ego massage may be great for someone low on confidence (although it will do them harm in the long term if there are skills they do need to work on but are never told this). For ambitious people like myself, this approach was worse than useless; not only had I lost trust in the manager, but I also couldn't enjoy or believe their positive feedback, and I began to be anxious about what weaknesses in my work or personal style there might be that he wasn't telling me about. For all these reasons, we can see why staying honest in your feedback is therefore vital, even if you worry that your teammate might not like what you have to tell them. High performers are motivated by their growth and by you investing in their development. You can do that by building on their existing skillsets and exposing them to projects that add more skills to their portfolios. You should provide them with responsibilities that help them grow and add more diverse experience to their portfolio of expertise. The best individuals are well-rounded and agile performers; people that you can shift from one part of the business and drop into something completely foreign to them and be confident that they have got what it takes to persevere, learn the relevant skills, and succeed. You can only ever ascertain your people's agility by giving them many different projects and roles to prove themselves. This proven track record goes a long way in their career advancement, and in ensuring their loyalty to you.

Shielding Stress

Another element not to be underestimated is that as a manager, you have more responsibility than your members of your team and most likely will be exposed to more stressful situations than them. How you handle these situations, and your ability to shield your team from that stress, is crucial. Allowing your team to feel unnecessary stress due to strategic or business factors beyond their control (and their pay grade) is very demotivating. Remember, managers, drive the behaviour of their entire team by the tone they set. When you come, and sit at your desk, don't forget that all eyes are on you and that each teammate could be trying to read your mood to determine if this is a good time to approach you. If you are visibly stressed and are flustered these interactions may not take place – they may never mention their great suggestion or important idea, and that lost opportunity cost has an impact on the bottom line, as well as making the team feel frustrated and disconnected from your leadership. One piece of advice I was once given that has always stayed with me is that to be effective in shielding your emotions on the job, one should emulate a graceful swan on its lake. From the outside, the swan seems to be swimming serenely along with perfect poise. Underneath, of course, the legs are churning away at top speed. If you can always keep composed no matter what, your calm communication style during stressful scenarios will be greatly appreciated and will go a long way towards helping your team stay calm and work towards a positive resolution of the situation.

Promotions: Taking a Risk and Getting the Timing Right

If you are an employer who values talent, you will appreciate that without that talent, your business will be limited and its performance restricted; you need to value your people, promote them, and take a risk on them. The chairman of the company that I work at now says something wise: Remember once there was someone that took a risk on you. No one ever knows for sure that they are ready for the next challenge (not unless they are supremely confident – bordering on the arrogant); what helps them face these challenges is a set of experiences that have helped them acquire resilience and expertise. As managers, it's our job to expose our people to those projects every two to three years, to wash away any complacency and continue their growth and development. If, after all these challenges, you see a record of proven success that indicates one day this person has management potential, then take that risk and push for their promotion. Don't forget that workers grow not just by obtaining a new job title, but mainly because of the teams and projects they become part of, the conversations they are party to, and the decision-making processes that they are part of. Once they are promoted it's important not just leaving them to get on with their new job, but to continue to support them. The support goes a long way, it will earn you loyalty and make them feel they can take calculated risks – a freedom which is highly sought after at a large firm competing against fearsome incumbent other firms. This has certainly been a formula that has kept me in my firm and kept me progressing and learning. My managers retained me by testing me, exposing me to different challenges, and, through that, helping me grow. Another important aspect of retaining talent is timing. Often you lose your talent if you haven't made them a manager or provided them with the right challenge by the right time. Regardless of the old saying, "Better late than never", it is more a case of "better early than too late" when it comes to retaining talent. Of course, there are patient individuals but typically, ambitious people are competitive and impatient. They may get itchy feet and remember you are competing with other firms who would snap that talent up in a second. Missing that window of opportunity will be very costly. Keeping those conversations active can help; talking about this during yearly evaluations, managing expectations, and delivering on what the talent expects, where possible, is crucial. There is of course some risk associated with making a move on their promotion sooner rather than later, but if you believe that person will be right for the job in the future, you may need to expedite it and support them now whilst you still can. Timing may also be the question of when in life should the person push for promotion. There are generally two windows; before you decide to settle down and have family, and when your children have reached an age when you can be more flexible with your time and other arrangements. If you don't plan to have children it may be other personal commitments, like caring for family or focussing on other non-work interests, that you need to schedule your life and career around. This statement could be seen as controversial, as some people do indeed have it all, putting in all the hours day and night to make it work with both family and work. However, if you want to have a work-life balance, I think it's reasonable to accept that the most realistic time for a pure focus on work is during those two windows in your life.

Moreover, I would go as far as to say that this is even more crucial for female talent. In my experience, women who were able to dedicate more time to their career before they build a family were more likely to want to return as full-time working moms and feel confident that they have all the right skillset to be able to perform their role upon their return. From personal experience as a mother returning to work, I found the first year after my one-year maternity break (diverse regions and employers will offer varying periods of leave) to be a real juggling act, to adjusting my work-life balance to new demands at home. Depending on which sector you work in, a year away from a fast-paced industry such as Finance means that upon your return there will be a big knowledge gap to catch up on. Thus, returning mothers need to spend time catching up, on top of adjusting to their work-life balance, not an easy task. My confidence (and I pride myself on being at the top end of the confidence scale) was knocked right down, I was rusty and needed to spend more time bringing my knowledge back up to speed. As a mother, I found it tough to put in the hours as I once did when trying to get a promotion, at the same time as getting home on time to see my child and husband. On top of that, I am grateful that my managers took that chance on me when they did. If women are not already in a senior role, they may find that childcare costs mean that returning on a flexible or part-time basis may not be a financially viable option. If my managers waited longer, I may have preferred to put the move up on hold until my children were in school. Becoming a senior manager as a mother of younger children may have taken too much of a toll on my family. By taking the risk on me when they did, they retained me. From a practical point of view, it's important to have open conversations with your employers and managers to get the timing right. Evaluate the talent of the group you have and think about who you would want to succeed you in your role. Ask yourself how long until that person will be ready. If you determine that they are 6-12 months away, you can focus during this time on developing the specific skillsets that they still need for their job. 'Developing' here may comprise as small a thing as getting them a book you think they may find useful; it may mean enrolling them on a course or it may mean delegating something onto them and guiding them through it. Introduce a process to go through this exercise at least once a year if not more, and ensure you make plans around it. Getting someone ready for management can also inform the approach you take during your one-to-ones; instead of outlining out how things should be done or pointing out certain mistakes your people made, it is much more effective when those mistakes are discovered by the individual for themselves. People are more invested in trying to fix a flaw they have discovered themselves, and this avoids provoking the defensive stance that people so often adopt when they receive critical feedback. The best promotions are those where people are already doing the role, just without the formal title and acknowledgement. They could be doing this either in the context of a parallel, smaller 'team within a team' as a deputy, or perhaps they have been covering for someone who has left a more senior role without being replaced. In all cases, they have been performing more senior tasks, delegated to them by their manager. Delegation is a wonderful way to develop people and spending additional time coaching those talents is another way of your investment in them. The time you spend with your top or most promising performers is the best investment you can make towards retaining those people.

Managing Up to Retain and Promote Talent

As a manager, another key element in retaining talent is ensuring that you are not the only person who recognises and believes in this talent. The way to ensure that is to manage your talent up within the organisation. Does your manager know what achievements your people are making, are you trumpeting these achievements enough when socialising with your peers to ensure they know about your people and what they can do?

Leveraging their talent is crucial, particularly for the end of year evaluations; if this is the first time that your seniors are hearing about the successes of this individual then it will be a cold sale, and any salesperson knows that chances of a sale are much higher one if the customer is already warmed up and interested. This helps retain people for two reasons. Firstly, because people (ambitious high performers, at least) like the spotlight and the warm glow of recognition and praise for a job well done. Secondly, and more pragmatically, the more people know about this person's achievements, the better their chances of being rewarded – not only in the short term (via end of year bonuses and raises being signed off), but also in the long term, when new potential opportunities will come their way and their names and achievements will give them an edge. One note of caution when managing up; there is a potential downside if you have raised negative issues with certain individuals to your manager over the year (or in previous years), subsequently proving that they have done a good job at the end of the year conversation may be tougher. The lesson here is not to underestimate the impact of the message that you are managing up, as it may have a dramatic impact on more senior people's perceptions and thus on later (re)evaluations and of that individual. Let that not dissuade you that managing up is a practical way to retain talent, however – we will focus on that in much more detail in the next Chapter.

Reward

One cannot talk about the retention of talent without talking about the main retention tool, which is the reward. A reward can take the form of direct financial remuneration at the end of the year, or a different role or responsibility that the person has been working towards. Let us not underestimate the power of money. It is seen as a dirty concept to talk about money as a motivation, but the reality is that the vast majority of people would prefer to enjoy their time relaxing or seeing family and friends instead of spending 45 hours a week working. So, every sacrifice has a price tag to it – but every skill set and experience has one too. Knowing the value of your talent is crucial, but so is keeping realistic expectations for salary, given the going rates at your firm for a person with equivalent tenure and experience. People do not like to operate blind, so having a broad conversation around the average range people in your role could earn will be positive. It gives the performer clarity, and a starting point for discussions around how attractive and motivating the proposed package is for your people. A good friend of mine, an excellent manager, left the company we worked at because she felt she was treated unfairly with her year-end salary package. When I asked whether she felt she had a good year, she admitted that it had not been great, but there had never been any precedent for her salary to suffer that much. Neither was our manager able to point any examples of poor performance on her part and therefore no good reason as to why such drastic reduction in her package took place. If her manager spent more time with her before, not only could he have better prepared her for the bad news at end of the year but also gotten her on board with the reasoning behind it. She didn't leave because her package was lower one year, but because she was disappointed by the way she was treated by management. Open communication can help prevent such painful examples from happening to your team. Similarly, in setting people up for success, selecting the right level of expectations is crucial. This is relevant not only to how you manage people but with the goals you set them as well as the role that those individuals hold. One area that is not to be underestimated, particularly in sales, is whether the target you have set your people is obtainable. If it is a stretch due to the constraints of the business environment, you are better off giving that target to someone junior who is going to be less impacted by it and bring that senior person onto some business where they have a higher chance of succeeding (such as running a big established relationship account instead of breaking a new untapped territory). Even if you may think that your high performer can change the landscape of this business, you do need to be vigilant when setting targets, as you will be taking a risk that could impact your top performer's end of year numbers, risking their evaluation and potentially demotivating your star performer. This ties in with another aspect, namely that some people are particularly ambitious and seek to accelerate their career faster than it normally takes. There is a need for such individuals in the organisation to challenge the status quo, but do not underestimate that, more often than not, that individual should be performing at the top of the peer group where they are experienced and proven, than moving across to a new role where they are the most inexperienced. They would run a real risk of being evaluated lower relative to the experienced members who have been doing the same role for some time, have already a built-up network of influencers to help them get results, and boast an existing pipeline of leads from previous years. At times this makes good sense, not just for the business, but also because the performer is so good that you feel confident in taking that risk. Nevertheless, it is a risk that should be discussed at length. Moving roles doesn't necessarily equate to increased salary potential, because if the organisation operates on merit then it's on the ability to achieve results and relative to others outperform them. As a manager who wants to ensure their people get paid, understanding which role gives each individual the biggest chance in getting paid will help retain talent and thus should be part of every manager's thought process.

Flexibility

Last but not least, work-life balance is a crucial component in retention. This is particularly important when managing millennials, who have grown up in a technological environment where it has been proven that work can be done remotely. As the world is ever more technology-driven and interconnected, many of us more often work outside usual office working hours, and outside of the office location. We check our phones on the train, we read the news, and dream up ideas that we want to realise in the office. If your commute is around an hour, which is average from central hubs like London and New York, that adds extra two hours to your day where you are working or at least thinking about work issues. Other than an enlightened few, not many companies, pay for these time hours or consider it as working hours, though I remain convinced that some of those hours spent thinking and working outside the office, problem-solving and brainstorming, are more productive and inventive outside of the office.

For me, if my team member needs to take their child to a doctor's appointment during the day or some other personal life situation needs addressing, they should feel that it is possible and should be encouraged to just let you be aware.

When my team members ask me if it is ok to drop their children off at school after a school break, thus getting in two hours late – I will always say, absolutely; this gesture not only goes a long way towards motivation (they are working for an understanding manager) but will also encourage this person to relate their working time directly to reaching their goals. If that means staying late or working at home to reach goals, then they would do it; knowing full well that when they need to honour family commitments or other important private life events, they are free to do so. Of course, if you see this trust being abused, then you put more boundaries around it. I think that any manager that doesn't factor in work-life balance as a crucial part of their retention strategy of their people is taking a very short-sighted view and will have real issues keeping hold of talent.

Since the pandemic, the meaning of flexibility and work life balance has changed. After a year and a half, where people worked most of their time from home, many people grew fond of this, and would struggle to go back to the office full time. In many cases this is because the pandemic has gotten people to re-evaluate their priorities in life. Where prior to the pandemic in many cases working from home seemed like a privilege, allowing for some time to be taken off work for personal needs, since the pandemic the level of trust has increased, amongst firms; awareness grew that working from home can be as effective as from the office. Arguably, that is only until everyone starts to return to office and those who are not back yet, may miss out from the power of collaboration, power of in-person meetings, the connections that people make in person and power of learning from others. However, working two/three days out of five at home is certainly flexibility that people now want to consider. On top of that, location where one works from home is another flexibility element that people are requesting, to fit in the sunshine and other family commitments (particularly in Europe). Post pandemic return to office policies are increasingly important when retaining talent; the clearer and more defined the policy is, the higher chance the firm has in retaining and attracting talent.

Managing during the Pandemic

Since originally writing this book, we have had the unfortunate events of Covid 19 pandemic, which saw the world working from home for a period close to 18-24 months. Many managers found themselves operating in unknown territory. No one had undergone training on how to effectively manage whilst working remotely, thus, many had to improvised. Hopefully, we won't find ourselves in this situation again, where we are working fully remotely, but if one cannot totally rule it out, it is worth reflecting on lessons learnt from the experience of these past few years.

During the pandemic, many families had found themselves having to home-school their children and still be on top of their daily work tasks. Very quickly many people suffered burnout and were experiencing high levels of stress that were not sustainable for a long period of time. Some practical examples of managerial tips that worked for the group I managed at the time:

1) Regular catch ups as a group. This helped people connect with each other and share their experiences and included both business and non-business-related meet ups.

Business-related weekly meet-ups helped to ensure that whilst working remotely the group still shared a common vision and goals. Personal agenda meet-ups (team quiz, as an example) made people realise that their problems were often the same problems that others had. Organising open forums helped provide a supportive environment with an understanding culture which helped boost morale. In the long run, I would say this helped retain talent. We even did a few virtual meet ups with families, which brought colleagues even closer together.

2) Empathy and flexibility. Many people faced extremely challenging life situations such as death in family, illness of family members or friends, isolation, anxiety, mental health issues – the list goes on. When this is the case, work can often become a secondary priority and as managers we need to accept that and support our colleagues. For some, during such a volatile time, work is the only stable distraction and, in fact, can act as an escape that keeps people going. When this is the, it's important for the manager to ensure that team members are not taking on too much and are taking enough breaks and time off. Offering time off, and supporting flexible hours of working, is essential. I know team members that logged a few hours in the morning and then again much later in the day, only after they had put their young kids to bed for the night. These colleagues were able to do most of their work between 19:00-00:00. One colleague was not available most afternoons but they ensured clients knew that they will respond at night. For urgent matters, they delegated, but overall they made it work. They were grateful that they could be in control of the hours they could work, and to make it work with their family needs.

3) Having regular check-ins with your people in a 1-2-1 format. Checking in on how they are and what you can do to help, is important on a regular basis. Listening to feedback and adjusting is just as important now as it ever was. This still is a new phenomenon that only with multiple iterations we will get it right. Not all meetings should be done on video conference – some can be just a phone call, and that phone call perhaps could even be taken whilst you are walking outside getting some fresh air. People who live alone found that they spent the majority of their time alone and were forgetting to go outside. Setting team meetings outside, or even doing a joint workout together also helped team bonding and grow appreciation from the team members.

4) Reinstating that we have a job that allows us to have a stable salary and a job with purpose, helped put things in perspective. If during the pandemic your firm didn't go under, and still managed to pay its employees – this is a huge bonus that managers should celebrate and highlight, and in so doing getting the group bought into the company that they are working for.

5) Reward: Recognising people for doing really well is definitely something that can help motivate and improve job satisfaction of those who have been working from home for an extended period of time. Creating competitions and rewarding employees with gifts such as Amazon or Deliveroo voucher, or a nice hamper package, goes a long way and is linked with outperformance. Working from home adds an extra challenge in how to ensure management are aware of what successful work is being done. It is very important that you, as a manager, communicate frequently with your own

managers about the great performance of your team members to ensure that your team doesn't feel forgotten.

Whilst the extended period of working from home may be behind us, I do feel that a hybrid model will become the normality. Thus, there may be months when you as a team may not come in together. Sharing one team vision, collaboration, and setting up group events is important and helps to boost morale and effectiveness as a team.

5 – Managing the Managers

In Chapter 4, and at various points in earlier chapters, I have shared lots of guidance on managing individuals as a team leader. In this chapter, I want to focus more specifically on how and where managing and developing leaders differs from managing and developing individual contributors.

Before becoming a sales manager (a manager of leaders), I had begun to think about not only what I could do for my team, but also how that could be measured and replicated by other teams similar to mine. In the team leader role, I had previously held, I had already created processes within my team and delegated certain responsibilities to my deputies (in so doing raising their game and preparing them to take on a leadership role themselves one day). Without these processes and delegations in place, I would not have had enough time to look around at how other teams worked, then develop and introduce the new left-field ideas that I had. By the end of that year, I was operating in many ways more as a manager than a leader. Looking at my business through a macro lens instead of my usual micromanagement perspective, I had grown able to entrust my reps to get the job done and do it well with minimal oversight.

However, when I became a sales manager, I didn't have confidence in any of my reports, nor did I understand what job entailed (although I had done many aspects of it well in my previous role – hence my managers' faith that I could transition to the sales manager role). As an ambitious individual, my goal was to understand all the processes, learn the business and simultaneously ascertain the quality of the people I had in the group.

Entrusting and Sharing

My style as a manager of leaders has always been to lead from the front, to meet with clients and get to know the business, to shadow people and learn how they operate and who they are, and to an extent, do the job yourself so you understand the ins and outs of daily operation.

The biggest difference between being a manager and being a team lead is that the team leaders need to manage from the front, and lead by example daily at an operational level. Managers in turn need to ensure that they employ quality leaders who understand what perfect operations look like and how to coach their team to bring results. You cannot and should not think that being a manager is doing the job of all your leaders, and you would be duplicating their role if you did it yourself. I found understanding and accepting this difference challenging at first. Another way to look at it is that as a manager of individuals, you have a greater daily influence on their execution. I remember, when I was an individual contributor with ambitions of team management, my then-mentor explained that to demonstrate my abilities as a leader, I needed to show that I could influence the results of the team, not just my own. My tactic as a salesperson was to compile a prospect list and diligently call off it daily until I sold enough to reach my sales target. My mentor told me to think about what would happen if everyone else had that list and we were making those calls together; wouldn't you all hit your targets quicker and close more over the year. Of course, he was right; by sharing this list (which was tough for me as I believed it was gold dust) I was able to give a significant boost to the team's overall bottom line – and more importantly, I relinquished control and trusted the group. Now as a manager of leaders, you too need to learn how to let go and trust that your leaders are having that effective influence on their people. This can be tough at first because as a team leader you most likely kept a tight rein on your business. Indeed, that's part of how you have been successful to date – however as they say, "What has gotten you there, may not get you here".

You need to consider what you are measured on and how you will ensure you make your money at the end of the year? Most likely, when you get that promotion, no one ever actually sits you down and tells you, "This is how to run your business, and this is what you need to do to get paid." In our organisation, we get given a target, both net and gross, and are then sent on our way to go achieve it. Even when the target is not met (due to unforeseen circumstances) you as a manager could still be hailed as having done a great job. Why? Because perhaps you have raised the team's overall knowledge or skills base significantly. Perhaps you have laid the foundations for major deals that may not have yielded results yet but look to pay out handsomely in the future. Perhaps you have hired good talent, fixed certain issues, or managed out bad performers. Perhaps you have innovated on a product and successfully executed its rollout. All of these falls within the remit of a manager – to think big, to build up a business, which is not a one-year job but a three-to-five-year one at least. This is all very well, you might say, but how do I know *how* to become a successful manager? Or whether you are doing a good job at any given point, given the long-run nature of these tasks?

From my experience, successful managers of leaders can set the strategy, get their leaders to buy into it, and steer the ship whenever the group needs to adjust course. When setting strategy, you need to be vocal and clear, so that if anybody outside of your group ever asked one of your team members what the group strategy is, they could reel it off, as well as outlining and defending the logic behind the chosen direction your group is focused on. Managers don't just set the strategy; they ensure that it is executed. Managers of leaders should have an overview of their business and ensure that the operational execution meets a high standard. The manager's role is to think about the group as a business, keep an eye on the profit and loss bottom line, and decide what factors need correcting to succeed. This might include personnel needs, product innovations or adjustments, re-prioritising people's time, training initiatives, improving operational fluency, sourcing helpful tools and technology – and the most important intervention, providing continuous help to the team to motivate and develop your leaders, which enables them in turn to develop the individual contributors within their respective teams.

Listening and Taking Risks

One of the biggest keys to success for a manager who is not executing strategy themselves in the day-to-day is listening to those who are. Observe the group's interactions, ask your group members open-ended questions around their experiences, and share those with your leaders before making a group decision on what action if any is needed to resolve any issues that came to light. Before making these decisions, you must achieve buy-in from your leaders, so that any change is not an imposition for above, but a consensus-driven reform. Let me give you an example; every time a person left my group, I would ask them about their reasons for doing so. Without fail, the topic of work-life balance would crop up somewhere in their answer. This was a common experience and reason within the wider company, but it should not have been my group's experience because (as seen in Chapter 5), as a manager I always made sure to offer my leaders that flexibility to keep their work and personal lives in harmony. If they were not, in turn, offering the same to their teams, then there is a disconnect and an unfair inconsistency. To clarify this, you need to run through scenarios with your leaders to see how they respond. If they give all the right answers, then the problem probably lies with the team's perception of how they would be treated if they took their feet off the pedal, instead of the actual experiences they suffered. Only you, as their manager's manager, can alleviate this tension and dispel the misconceptions, with constant reminders to the group that what you value and what you need from your people is output (results) and that you aren't necessarily concerned about the input (how they achieve them, or more importantly, having to be seen working 24-7).

To challenge this perception that my group did not offer work-life balance, I took a big risk in the summer of 2016 to test my theory that it was not the input that anyone cared about, but the output. The risk I took was telling everyone that they could leave work whenever they had finished everything for the day. The reason I call this such a risk is that I did this without asking my own managers' permission, as I thought there was a high chance my request would be denied (you could say I chose to ask for forgiveness after the event, rather than asking for permission beforehand!).

Interestingly, the bottom-line sales numbers didn't suffer, and nor did we receive any complaints from customers about not offering the same level of service as we did normally. A few people took up this offer a few times during the summer, leaving around 4 or 5 o'clock instead of their regular 6 pm finish time, but they would come early or log in from home to make up the time. One person – not a top performer – did consistently leave significantly early, but the overall impression was that many people still stayed way past 6 pm, completing tasks that they knew they needed to, to reach their goals. As a manager, I accomplished more than changing perceptions – I moved the needle in changing the mentality of my leaders which was a crucial milestone in their development. It is not the hours that matter, it is the tasks that get completed; and it is not how and where they have completed those matters, but the quality to which they are done. In todays' technologically advanced workforce, staff, and employers both expect that flexibility when it comes to working from home or leaving early and completing a task on the weekend – and for the workers, there is a big difference between working late because it is imposed from above and working late on your initiative because you want to do a good job and finish what you've started.

As a manager of leaders, you need to create an environment where the group is happy and motivated, and thus more likely to stay and work with you than seeking a change of scenery. A very important note: work-life balance doesn't just mean offering different benefits to people with children, but every person when they request it because they have made different life choices and we should not judge or discriminate against those choices. May I please leave early because my washing machine broke, or because I have a doctor's appointment, or because there is a window of time for delivery; these are all common requests that subsided during the summer of 2016. Not because these were not valid requests, but because people knew they had the flexibility to leave as needed and manage their time appropriately to catch up another day. And so, they did – people would casually mention to their managers, "Hey, I am off a little earlier today for this errand, see you tomorrow." They knew they could do so without any risk of judgement, and in turn, our leaders earned their respect and loyalty. Above all, I achieved a happy workforce without any detriment to the business.

Of course, like with everything, there are going to be some people who abuse the offered flexibility, but when that happens, you deal with it on an individual case-by-case basis. I feel that flexibility gains you more than you lose. In fact, in my experience, people who ask for time off typically will still find the time to complete their tasks ahead of schedule and most likely are putting in more hours into their work from home. So many people do nowadays, reading their emails and making notes on their commute and their mobile devices outside of working hours. We don't pay for that, but it is increasingly the norm and unofficially expected, and in return, the expectations of our employees have changed – they want that flexibility too, and we as their employers will gain a happier workforce by honouring it. A happier workforce means more collaboration, more creativity, and better results. This was my way to make an impact on my group – although remember, you should not get this involved very often. At the end of the day, your job is to empower your leaders to suggest initiatives and run the business smoothly.

Setting the Tone and Building the Environment

You empower your leaders by your communication and the environment you set for goals to be met. Your leaders have the greatest direct impact on your people as they spend more time with them than you can; so, remember, the tone and style you set in your communications with your team should ideally be mirrored within the tone they set with their teams. However, this doesn't always happen as you'd like, probably because leaders feel pressure to get results, to satisfy you as their manager. Consciously or not, they put pressure on their people to get them to perform to levels of urgency and perfection that they think they need. In my opinion as a manager, it is crucial that you are aware of what tone is being set beneath you, and that you make sure it is in line with your expectations. Let's illustrate with another real-world example from my managerial past. I once put a promising individual into an interim team leader role to test his abilities. This individual was hungry, ambitious, and an extremely talented salesperson. What he wasn't, unfortunately, was a good leader that could shield his team from the stress levels that passed onto him through me (a newly appointed manager). His team told me that some mornings he would come in so obviously stressed that they could tell it by just looking at him, to the extent that they were afraid to even approach him during this time. This of course is not desirable, an unapproachable manager could lead to a missed opportunity from an unheard good idea or unreported sales lead, not to mention how talent could get frustrated from this lack of support and this toxic, stressful atmosphere, and leave.

How would a manager ensure that a leader doesn't behave this way? Understanding your audience and what motivates and concerns them is key throughout. In this example, I should have spoken at length with this team leader about how he conveys certain messages to his team and tried to get him thinking about the effect that his language (spoken or non-verbal) and tone were having on his team members. After all, they didn't sign up (or get paid) to bear the stress levels of a team leader but are just individual contributors worrying about their targets. A good team lead learns how to effectively shield their team from certain pressures, filtering the message coming from the top to make it their own. They identify the heart of the message and translate this into what that means to their own business – whether it applies or not, and if it does, understanding how to pitch the relevant parts to their people.

This is done through ongoing coaching, that a manager delivers during one-to-ones. What coaching means here is talking through scenarios and situations, asking open-ended questions, and establishing an ongoing dialogue with examples on how your people manage situations. During your coaching sessions, role plays can form a useful practical exercise that helps your leader grow, for instance talking through how to sell controversial or unwelcome messages to the team that you know will meet resistance. First, this could be done simply by asking, "How did so and so react to this message, how did you deliver it to get a positive response?". Having this dialogue particularly at the beginning of your managerial relationship will help you ascertain the current level of your leaders. Coaching and scenarios analysis is done to see what tactics the leader uses to motivate their reps, how they deliver messages, how they set strategy, how they structure their team, who are their best performers and why, and what skill sets they are trying to develop in each of their reps. For example, let's say that the senior management team wants us to double our client visit numbers, have to book twice as many meetings as before. Thinking about the rationale behind such a request, the trick is to highlight positive advantages this will bring to the business and offer ideas on how to ensure that such change can be done seamlessly. In this case, something like: "Our customers are undergoing pressures from Brexit uncertainty. They will benefit from having us more on-site to feel our support during this difficult time. To achieve double numbers, let's be creative on how we book those visits…maybe we can invite more people in for an event or seminar and leave some time to meet with these people when they are on-site. What other ideas do you have on how we can reach those numbers more efficiently?" You can ask the leader to practice more of these scenarios and, that way when another potential troublesome message comes down the line, you know they will repeat this exercise and be better equipped to transmit the news constructively.

The Power of Prioritisation

As a manager, it is crucial to help your leaders understand what a priority is: what matters and what they could delay or delegate. For instance, using the same example as the last sections, you could add more guidance to a new leader in how to pass messages on, factoring in whether this is business crucial or a lower priority. You must ensure that your managerial rapport with the leader sets a calm and professional tone, one that never elevates the stress levels but rather calms them down. As we've already seen, they are likely to mirror this, so that they too could calm things down when they pass the message on. Understanding which leader needs more clarity around the messaging and those who already get it is also important because you don't want to come across as being patronising by underestimating their skill levels or leadership skills. As part of your mentorship, you do need to allow your leaders to make and learn from their own mistakes. Once you get the leader to see the effect a certain mistake of theirs has had on the business, they will most likely learn from it, because they made it. This is more effective than if you pre-empted the mistake from taking place. However, one thing to note here: those allowed, learning mistakes should not be detrimental to the overall business. When you are aware of a mistake brewing that is associated with demotivating a team or an individual team member, it is your job to spot it and step in to rectify it. Not in an "I told you so", or an "I cannot believe you didn't know this would happen" way. It needs to be done in a calm professional environment as part of your development session with them. Every leader, and every manager, has made poor judgements; it is part of growing as a leader and a manager. The key is to make a learning opportunity out of it and ensure that those judgements are then evaluated, and the lessons learned so that the same situations are handled better next time. That way leaders become stronger – which is the job and the goal of every manager.

Coaching Their Approach to People

Coaching your leaders should also focus on people management: how they motivate their people and how they evaluate them. I always ask them questions on who their strongest performer is and why, who is the weakest and what is being done to improve their performance. It is also crucial for team leaders to understand each individuals' strengths, areas of improvement, and career aspirations. Leaders are the ones responsible for having those conversations and perhaps your best leaders already do it. It is part of your job as a manager to ensure this is being done universally and to guide leaders in facilitating those conversations and career development moves for their individuals. We have covered the things they need to do in more depth within Chapter 5, in the promotion and feedback sections.

Preparing Your Leaders for Management

If (or rather, once) you have very strong leaders who are meeting your expectations in each facet of their role, and there is no more coaching on their role that you can usefully supply then your emphasis needs to shift to coaching them on how they can move up to your role, or another more senior role they have their eyes on. Managers can do this through delegating some of their responsibilities, such as certain strategic initiatives, and then afterwards talking them through how they performed, looking at how they did it, discussing their choices of approach, and how they could do it better. As a manager, you could also ask them to help your more junior leaders and get some practice as a manager of leaders with them. Coaching someone how to run a business, is not something that can be done over a single one-to-one, or through one conversation. This is done incrementally, throughout years of working alongside each other. Nothing should be done drastically or in a hurry on the back of your conversations. It needs to be a smooth organic process – discussing what works, questioning what doesn't, and brainstorming how one could alter it, point by point. Which alteration would be the right fit for your business and team, and which unforeseen problems or behaviours could this intervention cause? All of this is helpful for the business, of course, but also for helping the leader to grow into their role. You could share examples around what things worked well – or not – within your old teams; my trainee leaders always find this helpful. Then after explaining how it worked within my team, I would always go on to ask how this issue was being handled in theirs and what was the rationale behind certain processes used and decisions made.

When you are asking questions, don't quickly provide the answers yourself, but allow the leaders to think about it before answering so they ponder the significance behind certain elements of a task or job. The consequence of your discussion needn't necessarily be for the leader to change their approach (unless it needs to be done) but if you both agree that this change would be beneficial, remember to check up on whether the change is implemented, and if so, whether this has had a positive impact. Letting the leaders produce their ideas and not spoon-feeding them helps leaders take ownership of the change and see it through as their own, rather than something imposed upon them. This is something they will then also take with them into their new role.

Development

Every responsibility that someone fulfils during their daily routine, either as a leader or manager, can be broken down into discrete tasks. Each task could be coached and taught so that when it is performed, it is performed at a high quality.

Some people need more coaching than others. However, if you as a manager do not see any coaching being done by your leader, then pose the question of how they are developing their team. Even if they manage a very experienced group, development, and career progression are what people get excited and motivated by, and it is paramount that each leader has this on their to-do list daily.

For example, one role of a leader of individuals is to motivate others. The role of a manager is to coach leaders on *how* they could motivate others. A leader motivates people through understanding their ambitions, and the manager coaches the leader to ask what the motivations of each of those individuals are. A manager could also then ask, "How does a leader facilitate those conversations, and what are the questions they could ask to get those answers?". If a manager is more micro-focused, they could even ask the leader to fill out a form with the names of each team member, their motivations, and how these were being fulfilled. As well as facilitating such conversations, the manager plays coach by giving guidance on how to ask those questions. One goal for leaders to consider is to avoid making these motivational questions sound like they are holding an interview; to get honest and open answers about their motivations they need to be having this conversation in a relaxed collaborative environment.

Of course, there are nuances in how to employ open-ended questioning which differ depending on the experience levels of the leaders you are coaching. Inexperienced leaders may struggle to find the 'right' answers to some of the questions you may ask them, and this may be more frustrating than liberating for them and they may feel that you are trying to catch them out. At times, they may find it more of an interrogation rather than a coaching session. A good variation therefore with less experienced leaders is to start by going through your expectations and carefully outlining the theory behind the role, and how they could help people. Ask them about tough situations they come across, or how their business is going and their plans for growing it. As the manager of a less experienced leader, it is sometimes good to provide pointers instead of just waiting for your questions to be answered; it could be useful to help facilitate processes and guide them in what they could be doing to improve their numbers. It could be that you set them more short-term objectives, that you can check together and jointly celebrate milestones on. With a more experienced leader, you have open-ended conversations as previously discussed, and you also look at delegating more complex and important processes to them, so that they feel valued and rewarded with more responsibilities. It is also important with both senior and junior leaders to be the person that is always willing to listen to everything they have to say. Both senior and junior leaders have an open line to me when I am away on a vacation. Not because they or I fear they cannot do their job perfectly well alone, but at times they just call to update me on exciting successes, or interesting issues they are dealing with. They like that I listen and appreciate the significance of what is going on. If a manager doesn't listen, he or she doesn't get all the relevant information that allows them to evaluate them fairly at the end of the year, to spot areas that need changing, and ultimately to manage their group up (see Chapter 7). If you are a manager, at times, to drive behaviour where you want it to go, you just need to learn how to listen and to ask the right questions. Above all you need to be accessible and available for your leaders, they need to feel comfortable coming to you with anything and you need to ensure that this is the case. In doing so you ensure to be part of each problem and ensuring you don't miss a chance to help them succeed.

Credibility

At other times, of course, the situation calls for not just listening and coaching, but also stepping in with answers and making difficult decisions that will help bolster your credibility with your people. With your experience calling the right shots should be easy, or at least you will understand the key considerations that need to be thought of before a decision is made. However, in the event you don't know the answers, knowing who can provide them will go a long way, including turning to your manager if needs be for consultation. Being well networked in the organisation, with the ability to escalate and report up to major decision-makers could be a huge asset to the group. Using your seniority to be assertive with other stakeholders in getting your requests prioritised can also help. There is an art to escalating issues without burning bridges with more senior people in the organisation. We'll focus more on that in the next chapter on managing up, but the key is to do it diplomatically and share successes with others when you have them. Above all, you should avoid being the person who only ever communicates with senior managers or inter-department when you are escalating issues or fixing them. That is, you are becoming a nuisance and a demanding drain on their time, and the last thing you want when trying to make your name is for important people to wince when they see that name pop up in their inbox. Having multiple catch-ups with key stakeholders of your business, in which you make yourself useful and share successes will allow you to build a much more positive rapport. This way you build relationships and mutual understanding and encourage them to be more empathetic when dealing with your escalation. This is helpful in the long run too, as other stakeholders will want to help you and prioritise your requests over others, because they will know that you will not forget, and you will manage their name up as well.

Being strategically savvy will also go a long way within the organisation. If other people internally know they can rely on you to help execute their ideas, naturally they will go to you to collaborate. Managers collaborate and share their network with the leaders so that they too learn from those individuals and start building their relationships with these people.

Good Cop, Bad Cop

As a manager, you have to be both a communicator of strategy and the person who is held accountable for the execution of that strategy. Doing both of these, whilst enjoying your role with inspiring and motivating positivity, will be a winning formula. However, as a manager, you cannot always be the good cop. At times leaders will need you to escalate issues and make tough calls on performance management, resolve confrontations with other departments, push someone who is holding things up, and of course deliver tough feedback. With the right tone of delivery, examples, and useful advice attached, most people will value even critical feedback tremendously. Providing constructive but critical feedback to leaders is part of your job and in turn, it is your job to be able to provide similar feedback to their team members. Feedback both positive and negative needs to be provided regularly. As a manager of the territory, it is not your job to be the bad cop all the time. You spend far less time with the individual contributors than their specific leaders do. Thus, giving harsh feedback on your first client meetings or other collaborations with that individual may do more harm than good, in my experience.

Having said that, a big aspect of the manager's role is fixing issues where either the leaders are too inexperienced to fix things, they have reached a dead end with their solutions, or they simply need your weight behind a good cop bad cop strategy. Dealing with a tricky performance issue is a good example of when expectation and feedback can and should be delivered by the manager. The manager does play a significant role when performance management tips over in disciplinary actions or dealing with conflict. The leader supplies you with examples of the relevant behaviours and you draw on these and your judgement to deal with this scenario. During these encounters, you don't need to turn into Meryl Streep's character in *The Devil Wears Prada* – it is essential to maintain your friendly tone and respectful way of communicating your findings and action plans, backed with sound reasoning, and buttressed by examples of when your expectations were not met. Establish regular check-ins to ensure progress. If the individual is on board with the action plan and invests in all the necessary steps and corrections to make it out of this situation, they will have great respect and gratitude for you in the long run. If they don't, you have given them a fair deal and the best chance to turn things around, which is all anyone can ask for.

Your Mood and Its Impact

If you find yourself that out of your nine-hour day, eight hours are spent fixing issues, you do need to try and delegate more to your leaders, or coach them on only involving you when they need to. There may be times when coincidentally you do have many ongoing situations which are confrontational that means you being involved most of your day, do then slot some time to walk the floor and understand how everyone is doing and whether you can help people achieve their goals. Issues should not consume you, remind yourself that as a manager your role is to come up with a strategy, ensure you have trusted people who can execute, and your role is to motivate and retain that talent. As a leader, you manage a team of maybe 10 people; as a manager, you are likely responsible for 50 or more. The influence and reach you have is far greater, hence the need to remain conscious of your mood is also far greater. As we discussed earlier on, you need to remain upbeat and optimistic, as even if you believe you're keeping a poker face, people do sense when you're dealing with stress. Apart from the good reasons mentioned there for keeping a lid on external signs of stress, if your people don't know why you as a senior manager look stressed, it can spark wild speculation about the company's plans. They need reassurance that the world they are operating in isn't about to change dramatically for them. Even for staff who subscribe to the 'change is good' philosophy I advocated earlier, operating under a suspicion that changes are coming causes more disruption than excitement.

Managing Out

This chapter so far has assumed that as a manager, you acquired a stable of good leaders to manage. What if your new leaders are not up to the standard of your expectations? What if the leaders do not see the value of being coached? What if they once were good leaders but have become jaded in their roles or complacent in their knowledge and now have poor motivation and gaps in their product and market understanding? It is a no-brainer; your role is to either improve their performance or move them on. If your attempts to clean the house meet with resistance and you feel it is an unrealistic job, you do need to act quickly. There is no worse double whammy for the team members than having a poor leader and, above them, a manager who is unable or unwilling to act on it, as this has a direct impact on the performance of the team. Most likely the better members of the team are well aware of the poor performance of their leader and will look to their manager to solve the issue. If not, you run the risk of demotivating – not to mention losing the respect of – the entire team. In my experience, investigating an issue with a leader is much tougher than with an individual performer, and at times also requires a second opinion and deeper background information. One has to trust that when the decision was made to promote this individual, they did exhibit certain skills that your predecessor deemed important for the role. After understanding their reasoning (ideally in their own words, if your predecessor is still with the firm), you can make your judgement with all the relevant information. Perhaps over time, the skills of the leader are no longer a match for the current culture, skillset, or strategy of the team; then you need to act. In practical terms, acting here means setting out what team leader's expectations of their role and reviewing it periodically, as part of an informal performance improvement plan. If after three months your concerns remain, this is when together with your HR partner you identify what the next steps are. This can be either moving into official performance plan (which can have bleak consequences for any leader) or if you feel leader's skills are suitable elsewhere in the firm, you may choose to avoid performance plan and try and come to a mutual agreement, by offering them other roles (this can be individual contributor or leadership roles elsewhere in the firm, but only if you genuinely believe you won't be passing on a problem, but because you feel the person will be successful in that role), which are more suited to their skillset. These roles could be within your department or elsewhere in the firm. When outlining the reasoning behind the proposed change, it is important to share examples when their skills didn't match your expectations. Share what you feel this person's strengths are and why those will be valued in alternative roles that you are proposing. Often if you feel that the person's performance has not been to your satisfaction, they should be aware that this will not be the best compensation year for them, thus by offering another route, you may be prolonging their career and earning potential elsewhere within the firm.

If you have a manager that can be upbeat, proficient, a people person, and a go-getter all in one then you have got your perfect match and someone that can bring stability to any management team. In my experience, however, in big organisations, there is also value and room for versatility. Any leader that has been doing the same job for longer than four years may naturally become complacent to the extent that the team would benefit from a different set of eyes looking at this business. The leaders too will benefit from a change as they can become more agile; by not exposing your leaders to different challenges you risk robbing them of building up the new diverse skillsets that they can use to accelerate their career. Hence, as a manager, you do need to learn to manage through change and change of leadership.

Relationship with Leaders

In essence, with your leaders, you want to get to, a comfortable place of full understanding and respect for one another's roles and performance. Your leaders need to see you are invested in their careers and that you genuinely wish for them to succeed. If you are unsure about a leader, if you feel that that relationship is broken or you just don't believe in their abilities, it is in both of your interests to break that relationship, as the inevitable toxicity that builds up will be poison not only your management team but also the performance of the team as a whole. If your firm has 180 feedbacks, this individual will also not do you any favours when reporting on how you are as a manager. If you do have a good, respectful, and open relationship with your leaders, your communication with one another should be the same as yours with your direct manager. You don't speak to them or make them feel as if they are working for you; you have common goals, and the relationship should be a positive respectful one. You should still exercise your right (duty) to provide critical but constructive feedback – for instance, if there is an example when a leader misspoke, you could say: "John, the impact of you saying this may be so and so, and hence I would refrain from repeating that approach". The leader would appreciate it, listen to it, and hopefully not repeat it. There is a difference between being friends and having an open and respectful manager-leader relationship. You are not friends, but you should treat one another as if, once you are not their direct manager, you could very well be friends. If you have reached that level of relationship, it is a great achievement and a testament to you being a good manager.

End-of-Year Discussions

It is crucial to understand that you as a manager get no benefit from providing negative feedback to your leaders without constructive learnings or suggestions – especially if this is delivered to that leader in front of others, or even to others in their absence. This still means that you can flag up issues – you should have two or three areas you can raise for your leaders to sharpen up. The thing is that this should not be presented as a negative; everyone is always developing, even you. The goal is to make sure that at the end of the year conversations, your leaders know exactly where they stand so that there are no surprises. Your feedback should be balanced, covering things that worked well, things that could have turned out better, and how you see the following year working out. Other than maybe one or two points of development areas that are worth discussing, you don't benefit at all from making this a depressing recital of a year's worth of mistakes that the leader made. If it is an open dialogue throughout, then mistakes can represent healthy development. If the leader is repeating the same mistakes, that's a different matter and you do need to mention your concerns and perhaps stress the repercussions of these. Isolated errors should have been covered already, and no one wants to feel humiliated in front of their skip manager, this won't produce any useful motivational pointers, nor win you any respect or goodwill.

Raising Their Brand

As mentioned in Chapter 2, successful managers are not always the experts on every subject, nor are they expected to be in many work cultures. However, they are invariably expected to listen, and to empower their people to become subject matter experts themselves and build their internal brand on the back of this expertise. By this, I mean as a manager you can send your leaders on courses, on the back of which you will ask them to run a project that applies their learnings. That way they can become experts in the field through real-life experience or on-the-job learning. This could also be done by making subject or project advocates out of your leaders, asking them to prepare a senior-level presentation and own that piece of strategy. They may be reluctant at first, but in the longer term, they will be grateful that you are investing in their career development. It is the job of a manager to ensure that their leaders are working on their brand. It is crucial to not underestimate that everything you as a manager does with your leaders, your leaders can be and most likely will replicate with their team members. The influence you have is far greater than you may think. So, for instance, if you are working on raising your leader's visibility, they may start thinking up similar tactics for their best performer on the team. Raising team members' visibility is not only beneficial to the person whose brand is being shaped, but to the manager themselves, who will inevitably at some point look to promote those leaders and help advance their careers. Of course, as mentioned before no one ever cares about your career more than you, however, a successful manager should aid and encourage their leaders to create a brand. This could be done by little tactical actions like sharing a success story with other managers; or appointing them to a cross-team project that impacts not just them but others, expanding their visibility in the shop window. Similarly, managers should always proactively work with their leaders on carving their career path and helping them decide what that looks like and what milestones need to be hit along it.

Succession Planning

A leader should always think about who their successor would be; this is not just so you can concentrate on the career progression of that individual, but also provide business continuity for when the leader is out of the office. You need to have a bunch of people you feel can become leaders and you need to take an active role in testing them and preparing them for the next step. Similarly, you do need to have an open dialogue with other managers on how best to raise the profile of your current leaders, that way if they have new roles it will be easier for you to place them there.

Therefore, you need to have a team of leaders that you trust, you like working with, and whose career you are invested in shaping. If you don't have such a team you need to build it (see Chapter 4) and that takes time, but when you do and you will become the beneficiary of the creativity and autonomy you have helped them develop. Throughout my career, I have at times been fortunate enough to find myself managing people who once managed me. This can be an awkward situation, but it is an interesting one to consider. It will help immensely if that relationship was a healthy one from the beginning. That way when the power relationship is reversed, you can very easily mimic it. Why I mention this, is not to raise the prospect of you becoming manager of your previous managers – it is to emphasise that your direct reports could indeed one day become your manager. If you bear this possibility in mind and work backwards from that proposition, then you will no doubt feel incentivised to help ensure that this person succeeds and further, that they feel that you were part of that success. Indeed, this is in my opinion the definition of success: being able to help others succeed and ensure that they know you had a part in their making. A big part of making someone successful is managing their visibility and exposing them to different impactful projects that can provide them with the platform to succeed, from which they can make a name for themselves. We will look at this more in the next chapter.

6 – Managing Up –
Building Your Brand and
the Brands of Those Around You

The biggest asset of any organisation is the talent that they employ, particularly that talent they manage to develop themselves and retain long-term. A major contributing factor towards retaining individuals and developing them is the ability of leaders to recognise their efforts, reward their hard work and expose them to developmental experiences that allow them to progress and succeed. In a big multinational organisation, this task is far more complex than first meets the eye. By default, in a larger organisation, it becomes that much harder to stand out and to be noticed, because there is more competition, and more people competing for the spotlight. In organisations where promotions are not necessarily linked to peoples' tenure but based on merit and performance, making sure that your efforts are noticed, is the key to being promoted and rewarded.

In this chapter, I will first try to break down why managing up is essential across big organisations: both for leaders to manage up themselves and their contributors, and for managers to manage up the performance of both of their leaders and individual contributors. I will then go through practical advice on how to manage up because talking up your successes isn't necessarily going to be enough on its own to get you that promotion or inspire people to support your career; you need to learn how to manage up effectively to get to your desired goal.

Finding that Role in Your Own Company

People who are new to any organisation must learn their job before they start to think about different challenges, projects, or new roles. However, if they have already proven themselves, then why should they not be considered for positions where they can excel and gain further experience and exposure to a wider network of useful contacts. So how do you ensure that you are considered for the new role? Or, as a manager, how do you ensure that your people do?

When there is a new job posting, the manager filling it will want to go into the interview process with a clear idea in their head of what person they would need for that role. That is, assuming that there *is* an interview process. Unfortunately, you will often find that many new roles (I am not referring to graduate-level positions) do not get advertised or are not open for interviews. Many such roles are posted as being available in-house or even externally, only to comply with legal obligations; but how such positions get filled is at business level discretion. Very often there is already a preferred candidate pre-selected before the job posting is even made public. This is even more likely for a higher level of positions because the existing pool of talent is constantly being reviewed and assessed to ensure a smooth succession – this is where your managing up can increase the visibility of a leader or contributor to great effect. In some cases, the company already has a 'substitutes' bench' of people who applied to previous job postings, impressed the panel but did not secure the role. Once a suitable role does become available, there is no need for them to be interviewed again as they have already completed this process well.

In instances when there are no obvious known candidates, the formal selection process commences. Some companies are very proactive in advertising internal job postings, while in other places (especially some bigger organisations) employees hear about job postings informally either by being headhunted by someone who thinks they would fit the new opportunity or through word of mouth via their carefully built-up network of contacts.

Building Your Network

Getting approached for a role is flattering and motivating in itself, but above all, it is also proof that you or your managers have been successful in managing you up. It could be that an unforeseen opening at the firm has come up, and as the manager didn't have an obvious candidate in mind, they have turned to their trusted colleagues or managers to recommend the right person. Hence we can see that the bigger your network within the firm is, the better. It is also important to ensure that your network isn't comprised of just anyone, but includes people within the sphere of influence, people who hold decision-making power on promotions or at least have access to those who do. If the person who is filling the role is part of your network, you do stand a better chance of being considered ahead of others. If you are not on that person's radar, but you *are* on the radar of their trusted colleagues, then this is also helpful. Thus, the question is how to become that high-profile person that gets thought of for that role, and how to constantly stay on the radar for future opportunities. Getting on to someone's radar is not necessarily best done by getting onstage and shouting about your success. To get and stay on the right people's radar, you need to use appropriate methods of managing up. Many people associate the term 'managing up' with people bragging about themselves and their successes. The concept of managing up, therefore, becomes stigmatised amongst quieter, introverted employers who like to get on with their job and focus on what matters. This is an oversimplification, of course. Many introverted people have mastered how to manage up without speaking about their success because managing up consists of much more than that. Not only do most people not enjoy hearing others brag about successes, but actually few people feel comfortable standing in front of a group of people shouting about what they are good at. Instead, they would much rather someone else was praising how good they are to others. It is important to note, that not being managed up doesn't mean that a person isn't performing at a high quality and achieving results; it only means that their results may be overlooked and are not being praised as much as they should be. Particularly if the end-of-year assessment is based on peer evaluation, you want to make sure your successes are portrayed fully to get fair credit for your efforts. Awareness of how well the person is doing in their role will also encourage managers to consider them when they next have a new job opening, and to think about what the right next developmental milestone in their career is; hence people must be closely monitoring and are invested in this individual's career path.

Involving Others

To be considered for any role means that people are considering your skillset, which they may have observed by working with you, or heard about from their contacts because of the results you have achieved. Either way, it means that you have demonstrated your abilities and the results have been shared with others by you, or by someone else who has noticed you and shared their impressions with others. However, just hearing about someone's success doesn't necessarily put them on your list of potential candidates for new roles and new tasks that you will have to fill. In my experience, it is only when other people are close to the success story themselves, either by being part of it or by hearing the details throughout the evolution of the story, that they will remember you as the key player. How to do this without self-publicising? Involve people in your projects along the way and share the milestones with them, so they feel engaged with the challenge and share the excitement of your final success. Consider the challenge as being like a client engagement; in that case, you wouldn't hesitate to involve and inform other relevant stakeholders as you progress in those engagements. In my experience, in a big organisation, there are many benefits from not being the lone wolf when achieving results:

- Firstly, involving others means you are forming a team, which demonstrates and strengthens your collaboration and team working skills – a skillset that is very sought after, and one that will be applicable and relevant in various scenarios throughout your career.

- Secondly, by working with more people you are engaging with a more diverse and creative range of thought processes, and hence, increasing your chances of success.

- Thirdly, if there are hurdles along the way of a project, you are not taking all of the potential downsides onto yourself but sharing the burden with others who are involved and invested.

- Finally, by sharing milestones and initiatives with others you are essentially increasing your network and gaining access to people that may have more influence than your immediate co-workers. The more people that get involved, the more people become stakeholders with skin in the game, watching you and hoping that you succeed – and eager that you share that success with them. You are increasing the visibility of the project – and hence your own – not just with one individual but with many. In addition, having many stakeholders in the game also means that if you end up falling short, you share that failure with others, which is also important as it doesn't become wholly your stigma to bear alone. Of course, the flip side is that you share your success with others too, but at the end of the day, success is a success. As the initiator or lead on the project, you will still get the lion's share of the spotlight when news of your success spreads.

Throughout this project, you are challenged (or have the opportunity) to demonstrate your professionalism, ability, communication style, composure, imagination, problem-solving, and time management. It is as if this was an ongoing job interview. My definition of a project here can range from completing a small sale to an important task or even a large year-long implementation process. Regardless of the type of project, you must remain vigilant and remember the many eyes that are on you, especially those of the more senior stakeholders and managers involved. Each interaction you have leaves an impression that people will remember the next time they meet or hear about you. The most effective managing up happens when somebody from the group that you are working with, subtly raises your success to your boss, if he or she haven't noticed it themselves, which inspires your boss, in turn, to bring it to other people's attention. Ideally, it also prompts them to offer you another project or more responsibility.

Creating a Platform

If you are a humble, reserved character who doesn't like to scream and shout about what you are doing and achieving, you can tell yourself that if you are good at your job, someone is bound to notice and mention it. However, even if it feels right to you, and even if this is how things maybe ought to be, in reality, this is a risky strategy when it comes to effectively manage upwards. What if you currently do not have a platform from which you can shine? What if your job is mundane, and the same as what everyone else is doing, giving you little room to differentiate your performance from that of others? In this case, you need to think of something additional to your core responsibilities and deliver it. The three-step magic formula of success is to do your job well, plus doing something good that no one else is doing, something that not only impacts you but those around you also. Then, finally, you would need to ensure that people around you are aware of what you are doing. This is the formula that has helped me achieve the results that I have much faster than my peers within our large international organisation.

Individual Contributor Example

This formula applies whether you are an individual contributor, a team leader, or are a manager. An individual contributor tends to be motivated by praise, success, and by responsibilities that allow them to shine. Ambitious individual contributors may want to become a leader themselves, so that 'something extra' that they do on top of their job will most likely be connected to boosting their good professional reputation within the business. It is not unusual that they will also try and flex their managing muscle by seeking out project team roles that will impact their peers. They will be encouraged to demonstrate their ability to lead their team before they can be appointed a leader, hence their desire for a task or secondment that demonstrates their ability to manage without authority, as a testament that they can indeed be a solid leader one day.

Team Leader Example

Similarly, a team leader's 'something extra' can be to do something for the group that typically would be handled by their manager – taking additional responsibilities that showcase their ability to impact and influence a larger group. It is most effective when this is not assigned by the manager, but rather as something that the leader has suggested or volunteered on their initiative. If what they do has an impact on the bottom line and helps the manager, the manager should appreciate and praise their efforts, and share that praise with others.

If your manager is the insecure type, and you worry they might suspect that you are angling to get their job, it may be wiser and safer to look for these additional responsibilities not only within your department but externally – as well as reassuring your manager that you aren't encroaching on their turf, this has the added benefit of increasing your visibility and outreach to other management groups that may also be impressed enough to manage up your profile from your efforts.

Managerial Example

For a manager, that 'something extra' can be business or people related. After all, these are the two driving agendas of any manager. How is business going, and do you have the right people to ensure that business is booming? At a managerial level, managing up means doing something that impacts not just your immediate direct group but also the groups of your peers. It should be something that your peers will value and buy into, otherwise, you might not get the cooperation you need to be effective at such a high level. It is advisable to join forces with another manager to solve an issue that will benefit all teams. You also have more influence if you can present your initiative as coming from an advocate for the department. You may even become recognised henceforth as the subject matter experts in whatever field you are intervening in. This needn't be technological but could cover for instance the areas of recruitment, or people retention. A hard lesson that I have learned with experience is that typically, people think of a current organisational problem and try to fix it for their 'something extra'. This seems attractive as it is something that they know to be a source of real frustrations, a problem they know intimately, and an area where colleagues will appreciate a solution – surely it's a no-brainer, they think. The drawback with that becomes apparent once you ask yourself: "If this is such an obvious problem, why has no one fixed it before?" The challenge is that, very often, it is still a problem for deep-rooted historical reasons that make it hard to fix. Going into fixing mode will mean getting key stakeholders to agree that this is a problem – without their blessing any effort you may put into it may go to waste, or even cause trouble for you. Perhaps there is a long-standing valid reason for how things are being run, or a hidden agenda in the background, that you are not privileged enough to know. Also, even if there is a consensus that this indeed is a problem, the timing needs to be right for your intervention; resources need to be available, you need to get them assigned to your project, and you need to feel sure that a solution is feasible and within your capacity to achieve. The goal should always be a project that is not only feasible but fixable within a short-to-medium timeframe. In my experience, to be on the safe side your special extra project should be business-related, with a clear visible impact on the bottom line. That way, it's more likely that other stakeholders will see the potential benefits and sign off on it. Plus, when you have succeeded, this kind of benefit is more likely to impress stakeholders higher up the corporate structure, who might not care or understand about any process or workflow breakthrough you have masterminded.

Advantages of Managing Up Your Leaders

Managing up should not be driven by selfish motivations of wanting to get yourself ahead, but it can help you get experience and useful feedback that can help you develop. For a manager there are also multiple advantages to managing up your team leaders:

- Firstly, it showcases that you as a manager have got a strong team, getting you kudos for the right selection and development of your people. Spotting talent and helping them grow goes down well in any organisation.
- The team leader will feel valued and recognised, they will work harder for you and are more likely to have that gratitude and loyalty to you throughout their career. As mentioned in the last chapter, at some point during your career, you may swap seats with this rising star. Cementing a good working relationship early will go a long way towards making that an advantage for you. If you continuously manage up the performance of your leaders, they are more likely to

get hand-picked for other projects. Their confidence and skills will develop which will, in turn, help their performance within your group.

- In addition, part of everyone's motivation for working in any organisation is monetary. Raising the profile of leaders will boost their chance of getting better compensated at the end of the year, motivating them and the rest of your team (who think, "That could be me"). Hence, your whole team works well, and you and everyone else reaps the financial rewards for that. Everyone wins.

Once your leaders see and understand how you are raising their profile, they will hopefully learn from you and follow suit with their teams. This will have a positive impact on team morale, as their people get motivated by seeing their efforts recognised. Team members may also start being exposed to different projects and thus develop skill sets that will prepare them for their next challenge. If your leader doesn't have anyone to praise on their team, that in itself indicates talent gaps in that team, which should prompt the leader to performance manage more carefully and hire new fresh talent. Similarly, if your leaders do successfully manage up their people, they may get better compensated than their peers. This is good news, essentially because happy people work harder. Working hard correlates closely to positive results, and the leader recording a strong year's performance. Many junior leaders tend to focus on what their people can improve on, rather than what they have done well. This means that throughout the year the leader talks (and the manager hears) more about the negative or developmental aspects of their people, rather than managing up their positives. However, when it comes to getting their pay reward signed off at the end of the year, they change course and are suddenly talking about all positives. Of course, because they have left this effort right until the end, it is that much harder to sell the idea that this person deserves a salary increase to a manager who has heard only negatives all year. Managing up is, therefore, a little like selling internally; it needs to happen constantly until you achieve the result you are after for each employer in your team, which could be getting them paid more, promoted, or moved into their desired role. Leaders have to be mindful that their managing up should be consistent. A significant benefit that you get from successfully managing people up so that they get noticed and promoted, is that it opens up a spot for someone else to step up and fill that person's shoes. This progression affords you another person whose development you can have a significant impact on. In addition, it showcases you as a leader or a manager of someone who nurtures and advances their people's careers; an extremely sought-after quality in a leader. This makes you a desirable manager to work for, which in turn, attracts the best ambitious young talent.

Practical Tactics of Managing Up

I have now outlined the reasons why people need to think about managing themselves and their people up. The question now becomes *how*: what are the best practical ways of raising someone's profile? Managing someone up is not a task that you do to tick a box; it is an art, and to do it well, it needs to constantly be on your agenda in your conversations with peers and superiors; talking about people's performance and praising what people have done, why you believe it's impactful, and always have an example to hand. For example, after a meeting that involved a lot of careful handling of clients' objections, you would complement your person's performance, not only to your direct manager but to their peers. It is such a small effort from your end to just send a note or mention it in a public forum; but in return, you get a grateful employer who appreciates their manager for valuing their effort, and it also lights a fire under their peers (who are now thinking that they need to step up to win such praise themselves). The next time the praised person's peer needs help with the skillset in questions, they may now see this individual as the go-to person to approach. You, thus, set off a whole domino effect of development, and ultimately your manager will also associate this person with this trait and skillset and think of them whenever a different situation needing this skill arises. The communication part of managing up can be done via email; it could be dropped into a passing conversation, or during a presentation, you could drop names of people whom you know do a good job in certain scenarios. Too often, I find that managers do not use the easiest technique of motivation and development, by simply sharing other peoples' strengths and celebrating successes with others regularly. By the way, this technique makes you attractive to work for – after all, who wants to work with a manager who never recognises and praises?

As a manager, you need to see value in praising not only for your people but those for your peer's colleagues. The more you exhibit that behaviour, the more your peers will be influenced to start doing the same. By taking this step, I know that the manager, upon hearing about my praise of their people, may ask me to take a direct interest in this individual, and help support their career as an internal advocate. A second practical example of managing up is project work. As a manager, you cannot be with all your people all the time to see what they do well. You do want to facilitate an environment where a person can show you something extra that puts their performance on display. This could be a month-long strategic project or an advocacy role. An advocacy role means putting someone in charge of, and accountable for, a particular pillar of the strategy. The success criteria should be clearly defined, but the execution guidelines should be left vague; that way they will have room to surprise you with their innovation. Typically, an advocate does not have a position of authority, so this will also stretch their ability to influence without recourse to direct solid reporting line seniority. By facilitating this role or project, you create an opportunity for the person to shine and get results – and of course to report those results back. That last stage may seem the least important, but it offers a big opportunity for managing up. Ask them to add their line manager into the email chain, and to mention the results among their group and in group settings. At the same time, make sure you share their report and your impressions of it, to anyone you think would be interested (and influential). This secondment also hopefully exposes them to experience that makes them subject matter experts, so not only are you managing the person up, but you are also upskilling them and developing them in the process. Exposing someone to a different experience may also mean lending them out to another team, or another department. Again, this empowers that person to become the spokesperson on how things are done in a position that they have just left and bring this expertise to their new role. They will inevitably develop and become more versatile as they learn their new role, work with new types of people, and pick up the nuances of a new manager. It is key to stay in touch with them if this is a mid-term solution enacted as part of managing up. You can develop by drawing synergies between the different roles, and then managing up the successes from the collaboration. Above all, taking on a new challenge, and being exposed to new management and people, expands this persons' network. As long as they continue to deliver results, their access to a diverse range of influencers increases.

Mentors

Another technique of managing people up is through mentoring programs. An individual contributor can ask to be mentored by other people and managers, thus demonstrating their ambition to grow. Within my firm, when I was relocated to New York City, I felt that I didn't have relationships with many senior managers, so I proactively sought out a mentorship program to enrol in. I found one which allowed me to personally select an individual to be mentored by. At first, I thought I should select my manager's manager, but then I felt that I would benefit more if I selected the head of a business area I didn't know much about, as we were unlikely to cross paths otherwise, and thought I could learn something different from them. Little did I know that mentorship was not just taking some spare time to meet with a senior manager on the side. In our first meeting, my mentor grilled me on my work, what I wanted to achieve from that meeting and what I hoped to get from him as a mentor. We had no more than four formal hours together over the mentorship programme, but each hour-long session was a stretch; it challenged me to come prepared and made me think outside of my comfort zone. More importantly, after the program finished, I had gained an insider in another business, a person I could reach out to if I ever had an issue and vice versa. As I progressed in my career and moved back to Europe, I often got *ad hoc* emails from this mentor, someone now extremely senior at my company, asking me for my opinion, and looking for insights from the ground. Those emails made me feel important and valued. I was pleased that our mentorship lasted and was beneficial for both parties. I also know that if I ever wanted to change course in my career, I could always approach this senior manager and ask for advice, or even a job. This experience has taught me that you can approach different mentors at different stages of your career, depending on what areas of development you are focussing on. In my career, I have had many mentors, but above all one 'lead mentor', an individual that I have had a lot of support from in my career; who stuck their neck out for me and promoted me into various roles. I am extremely grateful and attribute a lot of my success to him. Mentorship programs are a phenomenal way to manage yourself up, but managers can also use them as a tool to help manage their people up. In your regular catch-ups, try to identify an area of development for each of your reps or leaders. Ideally, you would accompany this suggestion with your recommendation of another manager that they could mentor them on that subject with, someone who you deem to be good at it. Typically, this takes the form of a specific project, but it does not have to. A person could just approach a manager to say, "I want to learn how you were able to build your career." Or they could even ask them for input about specific issues, along the lines of "I'm working on this deal, but I'd love your advice on how to get it over the finish line", or even "I am having a tough time handling one particular character in my team – how have you dealt with this sort of thing yourself?" (obviously in that second example, they would need to phrase the approach carefully and supply any detail very tactfully). Personally, I am yet to meet a manager who *doesn't* like being asked how they managed to succeed or is reluctant to share their wisdom. It is also a compliment to the mentor to be referred to by another manager, hence you too might get a reciprocal call, to help someone that the mentor refers. Again, we see how your managing up to help your people ends up helping you as a manager to further your own network through collaboration. Encouraging your people to attend formal training courses or events also helps them. Working alongside people from other teams that they wouldn't usually come in contact with (often of a comparable level and career stage), is a great way to build their contacts network and start to manage horizontally. A simple example of this would be enrolling them in a training session with other participants, or a conference or other external engagement where there will be people from different departments taking part. Brief that individual contributor and discuss how they should approach this experience. Emphasise that they should actively take part – not spending the entire time speaking to people that they already know but going outside their comfort zone and meeting new people. They need to realise that any new engagement with a new department helps them increase their network, find opportunities to collaborate and a source of new ideas, and help them see a bigger company picture. I have personally been part of many such events which exposed me to many new people; this has not only helped me discover other talented people across our organisation that I can turn to for advice but also has unearthed talent which I can later seek to hire. Managing up is of course easier if you have a platform to do it from. if someone gives you a project to run, makes you an advocate, or selects you to part take in a training, you have many more opportunities to meet with a wider range of people to talk about what you are doing and why. It doesn't need to be talking about the results of the project; it could even be talking about career milestones or asking people for advice.

However, don't worry if this hasn't happened to you yet. Firstly, you do not need to wait for a platform to be presented to you on a plate; you can create your own platform by suggesting projects or volunteering yourself to take up advocacies. Secondly, having a platform is not the only way to manage up. Even if a platform is not available, or if you just can't do on top of your already demanding role, you could just focus on doing a great job in your role, and manage up by sharing results, milestones, or even challenges with others. This is the trick, alongside building relationships with other stakeholders of your firm by speaking to them and touching base with them at multiple points throughout your career.

Of course, the easiest way of managing yourself up as an individual contributor is to be a top performer that brings results consistently. As a manager of this individual, when they reach their targets, you benefit. You will then naturally celebrate their results, praise them, and manage them up. To be that top performer year on year is hard, as competition grows. As the platform from which you can succeed changes, all of the examples we've already seen will help you manage yourself and your teams up.

Finally, managing up can be done very subtly – but also very effectively – by just letting your team members run with ideas and encouraging them to manage themselves up. About 10 years ago, I had a meeting with a government institution where I briefed them all about the way we captured a generic price for a specific instrument type. I went into that meeting as a junior representative, simply sharing the methodology of how we did this, why it was a good measure, and who already used it. Two weeks later, I learned that this organisation had taken my explanation and used it as the basis for their advisory paper to the market, I was stunned. I quickly realised what my meeting and relationship with this group had meant, and the impact that it would have on our pricing methodology. Indeed, from this and later interactions with this client, I made a huge impact on the market and the profile of our services going forward.

My manager at the time (and longstanding mentor I mentioned), listened to this story and then did two things: firstly, he asked me to send an email to his manager, copying in that manager's manager. He then asked me to stand up in front of the entire department to share the success. He could have very easily done the managing up, and spoken about it himself, raising my profile that way. But as part of helping me learn to manage people, what he did instead, taught me the value of managing up and the importance of sharing success. Now, when I see that my team leader is onto a good idea, I often tell them that they need to meet with my manager and start building traction and buy-in for this idea higher up the food chain. I demand that this person involves others. It is much easier for me to do it for them, especially because I already have these relationships – but by delegating, you as a manager not only teach them the essence of managing up but also encourage them to increase their network.

Last but not least, managers should not underestimate the power of socialising, having that coffee with a peer or going to someone's leaving drinks. This is an experience for you to speak to individuals you don't cross paths with, and an opportunity to build or deepen personal relationships with people you don't know well. Having personal relationships with your co-workers, and even superiors will make the managing up process much easier and more enjoyable.

7 – Leadership and Management: Putting It All Together

Of course, it is not for me to judge how successful I am as either a leader or a manager; that is for my past and present colleagues to say. However, I passionately believe that to fully support you, your superior should be able to be both in different scenarios. Moreover, I believe, that to be a good manager you do need to create an environment around you that will require you to display leadership in multiple ways. In that case, you may be wondering, why isn't this book called *Practical Leadership Skills*?

Why Practical Management Skills?

The title I chose for this book is *Practical Management Skills*, and all three words there are important. 'Practical' because wherever I have provided suggestions, I think you will instantly grasp the benefits, and also be able to follow my guidance on how to do it. When I was a young manager desperately looking for help, the books I found gave me plenty of theories about what I ought to achieve, but not how to get there, or even why it was a good idea. With the logic, rationale, and real-world examples supplied around every hint, you will be able to explain to the team exactly what you're doing and why; because as previously discussed, you need that buy-in from everyone before you can all pull in the same direction.

'Skills' because I believe that great managers are made not born – and that I can teach anyone all the skills needed to become an effective manager. Many managers, including me, didn't go into management with any desire or aptitude for leading others but using the insights, I have provided in the book to complement your inherent strengths and talents, I am confident that any reader can pick up the skills needed to do this successfully.

Finally, we also have 'Management'. I want to explain why I wrote specifically about management skills instead of leadership.

Leader or Manager?

In my opinion, the manager and the leader should both be close to the day-to-day business, to be able to lead by example and direct their groups to success. It does seem that many people today believe that this focus on detail is the core of a manager's job, and it is a bonus if they demonstrate leadership too. For this reason, I decided that my focus throughout most of the book should be on practical management skills rather than inspirational leadership skills – although you will see that I talk about leaders and leadership at length throughout the book. I remain convinced that managers can also be leaders – and that it should be the goal of everyone in management to do just that; to not just be a manager, overlooking the operational activities of unconnected individuals, but to instil a sense of wider purpose and inspire them to share your common vision and goals.

Create a Platform for Others to Succeed

Throughout this book, I have provided multiple examples of how, as a manager, you can create an environment where people want to follow you, where you listen to people, and adjust your strategy on the back of what you hear. Previously, in Chapter 6, we saw how your operational day-to-day activities should foster an atmosphere where people come to you with ideas, to progress on their job, and for help finding other mentors and projects to help them grow their network. All these activities showcase how you as a manager have created a platform for you to become a leader to those people, and for them in turn to flourish and begin realising their own potential. I like making an impact by my contributions, but above all, I love someone telling me that I made them a better manager. This is one of the greatest motivators in my job. Another major point for me is that, as a manager, you can and should be leading by example.

Leading by Example

In one of my roles, the head of HR once told me that our concept of leadership comes from warfare. When commanders used to lead their troops into battle, they led from the front, sharing the fighting and the risk to lead the way. Similarly, in the corporate world, managers show themselves as leaders when instead of standing on the side-line giving instructions, they take full part in the struggle for success. They run the race themselves and once they have crossed the finish line, stay involved and cheer their people on. If a manager were stripped of their title, would people still follow them? If the answer is no, it's unlikely that they embody the role of a leader.

Selling the Goal

General Dwight D. Eisenhower was the successful allied commander in World War II, who then went on to be President of the USA. As well as winning his men's loyalty by sharing the risks they faced in battle, he also knew the importance of sharing the vision and rationale for going into battle in the first place. His quote, "Leadership is the art of getting someone else to do something you want done because he wants to do it" nicely sums it up.

Inspiring Followers

In my experience, I have often seen promoted managers bring their people along with them. I have found that, rather than the managers surrounding themselves with people to ease the transition to their new role, the opposite is more usually true; it is the people who end up following the leader. I followed my mentor – the person who first promoted me – into two more roles after that initial promotion. Following managers typically shows that you think you have found a leader, a person that you want to be led by, and a person you trust to do great things not just for the business but, in the long run, for your career too. If you are just starting as a manager it is to be expected that you won't have people following you in your career move – though if you are already a seasoned manager and you currently don't have people who would follow you into your new role this could also be an indication that you are perceived as a manager instead of as a leader.

Manager and Leader in the Same Person

If you are a manager, you communicate and you organise your team members, you are responsible and committed. If you are a leader you encourage and inspire and essentially motivate your people towards achieving a common goal. Can one person deliver all these characteristics? I believe the answer is a big yes. The reasoning behind it is simple. As a manager, you are exposed daily to a multitude of situations because of your varying responsibilities. One job is to create and carry out a strategy to reach your personal and team targets. All this analysing, planning, organising, and coordinating of your part of the business to reach those targets constitutes your managerial characteristics. Another job is to retain, attract, and develop talent. In these other parts of your day dealing with people, you may have to encourage an individual who needs a pep talk, reassuring them what a great job that they are doing. You may be recruiting talent or building contacts during an event or presenting your vision for your department to inspire others; all these actions show leadership characteristics. To apply this to your daily routine, as a manager today, take a blank piece of paper and split it into two columns. On the left-hand side write down all the tasks that you do that you see as operational and contributing to your managerial tasks. Then on the right, write what you do that is focused on longer-term goals and the bigger vision of your job; activities that represent leadership qualities. Do not feel discouraged if at this stage you have more management tasks than leadership, particularly if you are just embarking on a career as a manager, it is a journey, and these qualities will be acquired as you continue your development. I set myself these types of tasks to make sure I achieve my targets and other objectives; other managers in the same role may not choose to divide their time this way and may get the same or better results doing different tasks. This is the beauty of the managerial role; you get the autonomy in how you get to achieve results and achieving that success sometimes is not a race but a marathon. Some people that I work with within a day-to-day capacity will see me as a manager because we are problem-solving together and I bring commercial awareness to the conversation. There are times at the beginning of each quarter where I set direction, where I give credit rather than take it, and when I introduce transformational changes instead of transactional; all of which are leadership attributes rather than managerial.

A Typical Day at Work as Both Manager and Leader

To give an example, I'll talk you through a day in my working life. I spend the morning dealing with a commercial deal – this sees me get fully hands-on, organising next steps and coordinating others to reach a successful outcome. An hour later, I am coaching one of my leaders to be a better manager by working through a conflict situation with another team member. That afternoon, I meet up with some junior female leaders to share stories and tips from my career development – the goal being to inspire them to continue networking across the organisation. In the evening, I am flying out with management peers for an early morning breakfast with a client, but before that, I have dinner with my team to build team morale and to hear their ideas and concerns. Undoubtedly, before I go to bed, I will be mulling over their feedback and considering how best to address the most useful ideas or potential issues – it's vital both for my success and to retain their trust in me, to ensure that I don't just listen but also take action. Of course, during dinner I also relate to their job and try and show them the vision of their role and share insights on the business, to motivate and inspire them to power on towards their success. So, as you see, the managerial and leadership strands of my role are intertwined throughout the day. The day described above is indeed what many of my days, my weeks, and months look like. I am responsible for carefully planning out my daily agenda and being proactive about what I want to achieve in it, as both manager and leader. All the activities outlined were linked in one way or another to my key performance metrics. Dealing with a commercial deal involves generating revenue and coaching up reps on their sales skills. I book weekly meetings with each of my direct reports to learn more about their workload and help them tackle their goals. My meeting with the up-and-coming female leaders was booked in a month earlier when I realised that as an established leader, I had the chance and the responsibility to help tackle a topic dear to my heart; the issues of female talent retention and promotion and spotlighting our current female talent. When you read Chapters 4 and 5 about building a strong team and retaining your talent, you saw more practical tips on what is expected of a successful manager. In a nutshell, however, we can say that a manager's role is to build their daily routine around the problems they are trying to solve, whereas the leader's sights are set on the goals they want to reach. Looking at your daily activities in this light will help you see how you are spending your day (on managerial or leadership tasks), and help you determine how far these actions are useful to the goals you want to reach.

Importance of Self-awareness and Reflection

Many of you reading this book find yourselves in a new situation as a team leader or a manager. There are new responsibilities such as overseeing and reviewing the performance of your business unit, choosing and coaching new staff, meeting targets or key performance metrics, improving the skills, and advancing and the career development of your people (I provided more in-depth guidance on how to do this in Chapters 3 and 4). It's good practice to seek advice from mentors and coaches (see Chapter 6) but above all, you need to ask yourself some big questions. This book will hopefully inspire you to be a little more self-aware, to do some soul searching about your strengths and your areas for improvement. Think about who your followers are, who doesn't follow you, and for each group, think about why that may be the case.

Above all, have you set yourself up so that you are doing a lot of listening and coaching rather than giving orders? When you read this book, I hope you take on board the significance I place on listening to people, empathising and communicating with them, and coaching them through tough situations. It is my opinion that no manager can flourish without being open to other people's opinions and willing to challenge your own. No manager can ever be successful if they think that their style of management is the only right way. It is imperative to be flexible, consider peoples' motivations and play devil's advocate to understand how some staff may react or perceive some things totally different from you and other colleagues. The fact that you are taking the time to read this book is already a step in the right direction. It illustrates that you don't think you have all the answers and that you want to complement your existing skills and find alternative routes to success.

What this also implies is that you need to adjust your management style with different types of people, depending on their character and experiences. Some people do not want to be managed in the way I've outlined elsewhere; they want to be led. This means a less interventionist approach and providing them with more autonomy, and in your one-to-one catch-ups, they will most likely take the lead rather than you having to grill them for updates. You may not need to monitor what they are doing in their daily work very closely, as long as their results remain good. Whereas, if you are dealing with someone who needs managing more than leadership, you are more likely to set clear short-term goals, with clear instructions and deadlines. This approach is obviously way more prescriptive, and you would coach with less autonomy and provide more clarity and specific learning and improvement points with your feedback. I covered these points about different management styles in more detail in Chapter 5.

If you have been a manager for some time, it is very possible that you already embody some of these leadership traits and demonstrating them in your management practice. If you are blessed to already have good managers in your team so you can focus just on leading, then you are in a great position to concentrate on developing and demonstrating your leadership skills. Either way, "Great leaders ultimately must rely on a holistic approach to leadership – they must be both a visionary and a manager."[4].

No Great Secret to Managerial Success

I want to finish by comforting every reader who has found all this daunting. I hope to have proved that there is no great secret or complicated formula to managerial success – although there are no shortcuts either. I do believe that some people are natural-born leaders who possess these leadership characteristics already. Even if you don't think that applies to you, try to apply the leadership traits I have outlined in this chapter within your managerial practice – you may be surprised by how positively your people respond. However, although I would say that I possessed some valuable leadership qualities when I entered management, I only began to become a good manager with experience, by being self-aware and by constantly working to make myself better. With the right attitude everyone else can follow the pointers I supply to become a better manager and a leader to others.

---

[4] Mark Miller, "Why Managers are Leaders and Leaders are Managers"
(https://www.emergenetics.com/blog/managers-leaders-leaders-managers/)